Barrel, Pit, and Saggar Firing

Related Titles published by The American Ceramic Society

Out of the Earth Into the Fire: A Course in Ceramic Materials for the Studio Potter, Second Edition
Mimi Obstler
©2000, ISBN 1-57498-078-5

The Extruder Book
Daryl E. Baird
©2000, ISBN 1-57498-073-4

Creative Ideas for Clay Artists
Edited by Anderson Turner
©2001, ISBN 1-57498-122-6

Glazes and Glass Coatings
Richard A. Eppler and Douglas R. Eppler
©2000, ISBN 1-57498-054-8

The Magic of Ceramics
David W. Richerson
©2000, ISBN 1-57498-050-5

Boing-Boing the Bionic Cat
Larry L. Hench, Illustrated by Ruth Denise Lear
©2000, ISBN 1-57498-109-9

Setting up a Pottery Workshop
Co-published by The American Ceramic Society,
Westerville, Ohio, USA
and A&C Black, London, England
Alistair Young
©1999, ISBN 1-57498-106-4

Glazes for the Craft Potter, Revised Edition
Co-Published by The American Ceramic Society,
Westerville, Ohio, USA
and A&C Black, London, England
Harry Fraser
©1998, ISBN 1-57498-076-9

Answers to Potters' Questions II
Edited by Ruth C. Butler
©1998, ISBN 1-57498-085-8

Great Ideas for Potters II
Edited by Ruth C. Butler
©1998, ISBN 1-57498-068-8

Answers to Potters' Questions
Edited by Barbara Tipton
©1990, ISBN 0-934706-10-7

Great Ideas for Potters
Edited by Barbara Tipton
©1983, ISBN 0-934706-09-3

Potter's Wheel Projects
Edited by Thomas Sellers
©1968, ISBN 0-934706-04-2

Decorating Pottery
F. Carlton Ball
©1967, ISBN 0-934706-05-0

Brush Decoration for Ceramics
Marc Bellaire
©1964, ISBN 0-934706-02-6

Ceramic Projects
Edited by Thomas Sellers
©1963, ISBN 0-934706-08-5

Throwing on the Potter's Wheel
Thomas Sellers
©1960, ISBN 0-934706-03-4

Underglaze Decoration
Marc Bellaire
©1957, ISBN 0-934706-01-8

Copper Enameling
Jo Rebert and Jean O'Hara
©1956, ISBN 0-934706

For information on ordering titles published by The American Ceramic Society, or to request a ceramic art publications catalog, please contact our Customer Service Department at 614-794-5890 (phone), 614-794-5892 (fax), customersrvc@acers.org (e-mail), or write to Customer Service Department, 735 Ceramic Place, Westerville, OH 43081, USA.

Subscribe to Clayart!
Clayart is the "electronic voice of potters worldwide," sponsored by The American Ceramic Society. Subscriber-initiated discussions range from questions/answers on materials and techniques to business advice and philosophical debate. Visit the website and subscribe at www.ceramics.org/clayart.

Visit our online bookstore at www.ceramics.org.

Barrel, Pit, and Saggar Firing

A Collection of Articles from *Ceramics Monthly*

Edited by Sumi von Dassow

Published by

The American Ceramic Society
735 Ceramic Place
Westerville, Ohio 43081 USA

The American Ceramic Society

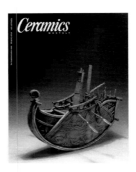

Founded in 1953, *Ceramics Monthly* is an internationally distributed magazine on ceramic art and craft. Each issue includes up-to-date information on exhibitions, available materials and trends, as well as profiles of individual artists, critical analyses, production processes, and clay and glaze recipes. While principally covering contemporary work, the magazine also looks back at influential artists and events from the past.

The American Ceramic Society
735 Ceramic Place
Westerville, Ohio 43081

©2001 by The American Ceramic Society.
All rights reserved. Published 2001.
Printed in the United States of America.

05 04 03 02 01   5 4 3 2 1

ISBN: 1-57498-127-7
Cover design by Melissa Bury, Columbus, Ohio.
Cover image: "Porcelain vase" by Rebecca Urlacher.

For more information on ordering books published by The American Ceramic Society, subscribing to our publications—including *Ceramics Monthly*— or to request a publications catalog, please call (614) 794-5890 or visit our online bookstore at <www.ceramics.org>.

PREFACE

This book was created in response to a growing interest in pit firing and related techniques in the pottery-making community, as reflected in ceramic art shows and in the ceramic art press. As issues of function have decreased in importance in the minds of the public and potters alike, and the line between pottery and art has blurred, such firing methods cease to be thought of as "alternative" or "experimental." Potters, ceramic artists, and sculptors wish to use whatever forming, decorating, and firing techniques are necessary to articulate their vision.

The articles included in this book were carefully selected from the pages of *Ceramics Monthly* magazine to illustrate the multiplicity of approaches to barrel, pit, and saggar firing. Herein are works of art ranging from wheel-thrown and coil-built pots to complex sculptures, tied together by a similarity in the firing process. Some of the articles were chosen because they illuminate the basic or "standard" version of barrel, pit, or saggar firing; others to illustrate variations on the theme; and still others to demonstrate some of the techniques used to create pottery or sculpture destined for the pit or the saggar.

It is the earnest hope of the editors of The American Ceramic Society, *Ceramics Monthly* magazine, and of this book that artists, teachers, students, and collectors alike will find value in these pages. Whether that is by ceramic artists and students as inspiration for new work, or by teachers as a source of ideas for projects or workshops, or by pottery aficionados as a stepping stone to greater understanding of the art, we hope it brings enjoyment to all who read it.

—Sumi von Dassow

CONTENTS

CHAPTER 5: RETURNING TO THE ROOTS: BURNISHING AND BLACK FIRING

CHAPTER 6: FORMING TECHNIQUES FOR PIT AND SAGGAR FIRING

CHAPTER 7: PLAYING WITH FIRE: EXPERIMENTAL KILNS AND RELATED FIRING METHODS

INTRODUCTION
The Allure of Pit and Saggar Firing

Since the first fired clay pot was made, perhaps accidentally by leaving a mud-lined basket too close to a fire, the potter has had fire as an active collaborator. During the millennia since then, progress in pottery technology has usually meant taming the fire—making it hotter, cleaner, more controlled, and more predictable. In much of the world, firing on the open ground gave way to firing inside a pit, then kilns were built to contain the fire. Refinements including chimneys and air intakes to improve air flow and control the temperature and atmosphere; fireboxes to separate the fuel from the ware; and saggars to protect the ware from the smoke, all served to reduce the direct contact of fire with clay. The ultimate advance in this direction, the electric kiln, allows the potter to apply heat to clay without requiring any flame at all. For many potters, this advance has eased the task of creating functional pottery; it has opened up the pursuit of pottery to many as a hobby, removed much of the stress of firing delicate work, and furthered the development of beautiful new glaze types.

However, along with the stress, the electric kiln has removed much of the excitement of firing, the sense of having an inanimate and unpredictable collaborator, and the eager anticipation attending a kiln opening. If the flame and the smoke aren't present to ruin pots, neither are they there to enhance them. Thus, since the electric kiln has become ubiquitous and indispensable, interest has mounted in alternative firing methods involving fuel and flame. This interest has extended in two directions. Though time-consuming and labor-intensive, high-temperature wood-firing has captured the enthusiasm of many potters. In a wood kiln, the element of the unpredictable comes to play in the way the fire colors glazes applied before firing, as well as in allowing the ash produced in firing to form a glaze wherever it lands on the

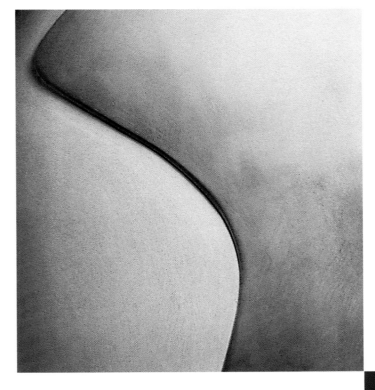

unglazed pottery. In either case, the result is fully vitreous, glazed or partially glazed pottery.

Other potters have taken quite a different approach to playing with fire. Potters working without a kiln at all, without glazes, arranging fuel and ware on the ground or in simple containers, can produce beautiful works of art colored only by smoke and fumes. While Native American or African potters firing in the open without electricity or kilns may regard smoke marks as a defect, many potters from industrialized countries are delighted with precisely such unpredictable effects and seek to capture them in a variety of firing methods. Along with the growing popularity of raku, the last quarter of the 20th century has seen experimentation with firing in pits and barrels packed with sawdust, newspaper, pine needles, and other combustibles. The saggar, invented to protect glazed pottery from the sulphur produced by coal-burning kilns, now has a new function—packed with pottery, combustibles, and volatile materials, and placed inside a gas kiln, it brings back the drama of firing.

Whether in a pit or a barrel, or in a saggar inside a gas kiln, the firing methods under discussion have several features in common. They are generally low-temperature techniques, not usually requiring large amounts of time, fuel, or manpower. The low temperature and usually short firing time means that the results of a firing are known quickly, and firings can take place frequently. They do not involve glaze, relying on smoke and volatile materials for effect. Thus, the resulting pots are decorative rather than functional, and relatively fragile. This means, however, that such a firing may take place with less preparation time. In addition, the equipment requirements are minimal and easy to improvise. Low-temperature smoke firing can be adapted to fire one piece at a time, or many. The investment in a single firing is smaller, allowing the potter to indulge in the urge to experiment. All of these features make this type of firing an attractive possibility for many who would like to collaborate with fire but do not have access to an wood-burning kiln.

Pit and saggar firing are versatile techniques. There is no right or wrong firing technique, no correct outcome. Success or failure are entirely subjective concepts. The variables involved in pit and saggar firing are so many: the types of clay and fuel; the size, surface and bisque temperature of the ware to be fired; the climate and the condition of the earth into which the pit is dug; the type and size of barrel or saggar; and other differences from one potter to another, often render futile any attempt to duplicate exactly another's results. Therefore, there are as many ways of pit and saggar firing as there are potters. Each potter who begins working in this evolving field embarks on a journey of discovery, guided by the happy accident, on which a personal style of firing is developed. The artists profiled in the following pages combine the elements of pottery, combustible materials, and flame in unique ways that satisfy their own aesthetic sense. Reading about their discoveries may inspire some to embark on their own journey; others may simply realize a greater appreciation for the effort which went into creating each beautiful or intriguing work of earth and fire.

If you are reading this book because you are interested in trying some of these firing methods, you may find it helpful to consider your own circumstances and the types of clay, equipment and fuel at your disposal. Before you read about the (perhaps bewildering) variety of possible firing techniques, I offer a brief section of questions and answers to help with this process of sorting out the possibilities.

Which Kind of Firing is Right for You?

Your choice of firing method depends either on your circumstances or the particular effect you desire. If you have access to a beach and can get permission to dig a pit and fire there, pit firing is fun and exciting. If you want to fire a small number of pots at one time, or can't dig a pit, you may want to try a barrel or saggar firing. If you have concerns about annoying the neighbors with smoky outdoor firings, or you want greater control over the results of each firing, saggar firing may be your best option. If you are not sure whether you want to fire in a pit, a barrel, or a saggar the following questions and answers will help you decide.

What are the best choices for color development?

A protracted firing in a pit or a large brick chamber, such as Peter Gibbs describes, will give the best chance for color development. Edge Barnes and Zoie Holtzknecht add copper to produce red flashing, in the form of copper sulfate and wire. For yellow colors they sprinkle salt and baking soda into the pit. Carol Molly Prier uses copper carbonate instead of sulfate, and adds seaweed to her pits as another source of salt. Other possible treatments for interesting color development are spraying or soaking bisqueware in solutions of cobalt or iron sulfate, as Gibbs does. To vary the results from pot to pot within a single pit, Embree de Persiis places pierced pieces of stovepipe over pots in the pit. Barnes and Holtzknecht may use steel or clay bowls as saggars for individual pots, or wrap pots in newspaper to hold various combustible and volatile materials close to the pot's surface. Rebecca Urlacher speeds up her pit firings a bit by setting preheated pots onto a bed of hot coals covered with additional fuel and volatile materials.

Pit firing is a great project for classes, workshops, and cooperative groups since a pit can be as large as needed and there will be plenty of work for all. Pit firing can be used for a small number of pots, as well, simply by digging a smaller pit. However, digging a pit each time you have a few pots to fire, then filling it in and removing ashes and coals afterwards means preparation and cleanup become a time-consuming chore for an individual potter. Digging a permanent pit or building a firing chamber can solve this problem, but you may then have to wait for enough pots to fill it up before you can fire.

What if I want color but don't have a place to dig a pit or room to build a brick chamber?

You can achieve a similar look working on a smaller scale in a barrel or can with air-holes punched in. Before firing pots in any such container it should be prepared by building a fire in it to burn off any volatile materials it may have been coated with. Since such a firing won't get as hot nor last quite so long as in a large pit, it is possible to encourage color development by spraying a copper matte solution on pots before firing, as Jeff Kell does. Glenn Spangler soaks wood shavings in soluble materials, including copper sulfate and fabric paint, before loading shavings and pots into a can for firing.

Barrel or can firing is ideal for small batches of one to several pots, and containers of various sizes—from an oil drum or garbage can, to a popcorn tin— can be used. Since the cans are permanent firing chambers, setup and cleanup time may be reduced over pit firing, though for a group of potters with a large number of pots it may be tedious to prepare enough cans and barrels.

How can I achieve the effect of a pit firing if open burning is not feasible?

If you have a gas kiln you can place your work in a saggar, along with combustible and volatile materials, and fire to a relatively low temperature. R. Bede Clarke applies soluble materials directly to bisqueware by brushing, spraying, pouring or dipping. Ruth Allan uses wire and filings of various metals, and even masking tape, to enhance color.

Traditionally, a large lidded clay cylinder is made to serve as a saggar (see p.57 for saggar clay recipe). Clay or stainless steel bowls, or even terra cotta flower pots, can serve as ready-made saggars. Clarke and Allan find it simpler and more versatile to build a saggar of bricks around the pots inside the kiln. Elisabeth Anderson dispenses with the saggar, by firing inside out—she applies salt and wire to the outer surface of her pots, then fills them with sawdust before firing in a kiln. If smokestack emissions of saggar firing are a problem, Macy Dorf offers suggestions for smoke-free saggar firing.

How can I achieve smoke markings without added color?

Random markings from swirling smoke are easy to produce, and the firing needn't be very hot or very lengthy. Rebecca Urlacher, for example, smokes some of her forms using crumpled newspaper in a metal can for just two minutes before pulling the pieces out of the fire. Jerry Caplan also smokes his pots with newspaper for only a few minutes, though he uses a stream of forced air to raise the temperature of the fire.

If newspaper smoking doesn't produce an interesting enough surface, pots can be buried in sawdust or wood shavings in a barrel or brick chamber, set alight with the aid of crumpled newspaper, kindling, and charcoal lighter fluid. Depending on the size of the container, a sawdust fire may burn overnight before going out. Sawdust-fired pots may emerge almost black, or merely marked with a few dark clouds—the variables being the type of clay, temperature to which it was bisqued, how much air gets into the firing chamber, and how thoroughly the sawdust burns. Jane Perryman fires this way to allow carbon to penetrate deeply into the clay.

Smoke-markings can also be produced by firing pots in a saggar in a gas kiln. Dick Lehman has developed a uniquely controlled firing process in which he is able to print the silhouettes of vegetation onto his pots in a sawdust-filled saggar. Marsha Judd fires in a brick saggar using manure as her fuel, and her sense of smell to let her know when to shut off the kiln. It is also possible to do the same thing using sawdust or wood shavings. The firing is essentially the same as saggar firing for color, without the need for adding volatile materials or oxides.

How can I produce completely black pots?

Curiously enough, a perfectly black surface can be the most difficult to achieve. Often a sawdust firing will produce pots that are almost all black, but achieving a uniformly black surface this way is hit-or-miss. Blackening a pot depends on building a fire hot enough to allow carbon to penetrate the clay, then smothering the fire so the clay doesn't reoxidize. Marsha Judd embeds her pots in manure in a saggar, and fires until the manure smokes but hasn't yet burned away. This is similar in technique to a sawdust firing—the difference is that manure naturally creates a heavy ash, which prevents oxygen from reaching the pots.

Often, however, it is best to isolate the clay from the fuel so the smoke can reach all parts of the pot and there is no danger that unburned fuel will blanket some part of the pot and keep it from becoming black. Michael Wisner has developed two ways to accomplish this. To fire outside, he stacks pots on firing stands over sawdust, then covers the stack with a barrel. He builds a fire around the barrel, to create enough heat to cause the sawdust inside to smoke. Alternatively, he can stack pots the same way inside a gas kiln, using a metal barrel as a saggar. I wrap pots in newspaper and then in tin foil, and fire in a kiln just until the newspaper smokes, which I refer to as a "modified saggar firing."

Trickiest of all is a silvery black surface. This can be encouraged by firing with damp fuel, so Judd sometimes dampens some of the manure in her saggar. If the silvery surface develops, it's great; if not, the pots are still a rich, deep black. Wisner's secret to the coveted silvery color is to burnish with graphite.

What Type of Clay Should You Use?

There is, of course, no one type of clay that will work best for the many different types of low-temperature smoke firing. Some potters use porcelain for the whiteness; others use a buff clay for a little extra color. For some effects, a red clay is most desirable. A raku-type clay may be appropriate, if the firing will be quick, to reduce firing losses. Though pit, barrel, and saggar firing are all low-temperature techniques, it does not necessarily follow that a low-temperature clay is best. You will want to select the clay according to the type of firing you plan to do, and the effects you want to achieve—though if you have a favorite clay, it may be equally appropriate to experiment with a variety of firing methods to find the one that suits the clay best.

What type of clay is best for color development?

You will want a white or light-colored clay. A red clay will not show the subtle colors from copper and salt. Carol Molly Prier prefers a buff to tan clay body to develop darker oranges and reds. On the other hand, Rebecca Urlacher pit fires porcelain, and Glenn Spangler also uses porcelain for subtle color development from soluble materials. If you insist on using porcelain for its whiteness, you may have to accept a few losses from thermal shock, or carefully preheat pots before placing them in a pit or barrel. After having experienced a great number of such firing losses, Ruth Allan offers some suggestions for protecting porcelain from the stresses of sawdust firing in a saggar. Jeff Kell uses a heavily grogged sculpture clay to make his large forms, which are fired in a barrel.

Most potters bisque fire their pots before subjecting them to a pit or saggar fire, both to protect the pots from thermal shock and to ensure that the pots have been fired to sufficient hardness. The temperature of the bisque fire is usually between cone 012 and cone 06—the lower temperature is preferable if the pots have been burnished. If the bisque temperature is too high, the clay will be less receptive to color development. Thus, stoneware clay will tend to give better results than low-fire clay, because it will be less vitrified after bisque firing.

What type of clay is best for smoke firing *without* added colorants?

The same types of clays that work for pit firing will also work for smoking pots. Since you won't be concerned with developing colors from copper, salt, or sulfates you can choose a darker clay. Smoke markings on red clay can look very dramatic, though a white clay will show a greater range of grays and browns from the smoke. Just as for a pit firing, a stoneware clay bisqued between cone 012 and 06 will pick up more color than a clay bisqued to maturity. It is especially important to bisque fire pots first if you will be using only newspaper for smoking, since a newspaper fire will not achieve high temperatures.

Many potters who smoke fire like to burnish their pots, or at least smooth the surface with a rubber kidney rib. A smooth surface will stand up to close inspection better than a rough one, and the subtle cloud-like markings of smoke invite close observation. Therefore, a relatively smooth clay, allowing ease of burnishing, may be a good choice.

What type of clay is best for black firing?

I use a smooth cone 6 red clay for burnishing and black firing because it is easy to handbuild, is durable even when fired to quite a low temperature, burnishes well, and reduces to a rich black color. On the other hand, Michael Wisner uses a low-fire white clay, because it most closely duplicates the clay used by the Pueblo potters with whom he has studied. Marsha Judd uses a red earthenware and adds 5% pyrophyllite to achieve a brilliantly burnished surface. Clearly, there is some room for experimentation and personal preference—though a high-fire white clay or porcelain is not the best choice if a reasonable fired strength is desired.

For the best results when black firing, pots should be unbisqued or bisqued to a very low temperature such as cone 018. In general, to blacken pots completely, it is preferable to separate the pot from the combustible material so only the smoke reaches the clay. Thus, the pot doesn't reach the intensity of temperature of a pit fire, where the pot is nestled directly in sawdust. If a pot has been bisque fired at a temperature much higher than that attained in the black firing, it will not be receptive to the smoke. Therefore, your choice of clay needs to be influenced by the fired strength of the clay at such a low bisque temperature. In my experience, a white clay is not quite as strong as a red one, and a low-fire clay needs to be fired close to maturity—certainly higher than cone 018—before it achieves sufficient hardness.

Though it is not necessary to burnish a pot before blackening it, a burnished pot will appear blacker than an unburnished pot. If you do want to burnish, your choice of clay will be determined in part by ease of burnishing and the degree of

Introduction

shine attainable with the various clays available to you. Clay bodies vary greatly in this regard but it is safe to say that a smooth body will be easier to burnish than a coarse one. Having tried to burnish many clay bodies, I have found that due to the non-clay materials added to lower their maturing temperature, low-fire bodies tend to be soft and chalky and difficult to burnish without scratching.

THE ROOTS OF PIT FIRING:
Raku meets American Indian pottery
and a new American firing technique is born

Modern pit firing evolved from a movement beginning in the 1960s toward appreciating pottery as a pre-industrial process, to get back to the basics of pottery. After the publication of Bernard Leach's *A Potter's Book,* American potters became intrigued with the Japanese technique of raku, seeing it as a more immediate pottery experience than firing in a standard kiln. In the 1970s, ambitious raku and wood-fired pottery workshops led participants to make pots from native clay and bisque fire them in large pits prior to glazing and refiring them in brick or stone kilns built on the spot. An appreciation for the smoke markings on the bisqued pots prompted some participants to stop short of the glazing part of the process.

During this same time, the urge to practice and teach pottery as a non-industrial art "experience" led to a growing interest in American Indian pottery techniques. Potters were encouraged to dig their own clay, form pots without a wheel, decorate them by burnishing or incising, and fire them on the open ground to gain a holistic understanding of the process. Early practitioners of raku in America, such as Hal Riegger, were also active in experimenting with firing on the open ground or in pits as a way to develop insight into early potters' first advances beyond the bonfire.

Since then, pit firing has gone from being part of a spiritual or meditative process leading to a greater understanding of the earth and what it means to be a potter, to a process undertaken for the sake of its uniquely beautiful product. As potters and the consuming public grow away from the notion of function to accept that pots need not even pretend to be usable, alternative firing styles that result in entirely non-functional ware have increased in popularity.

Raku, as practiced in America, grew to resemble Japanese raku very little. Where Japanese raku pottery is quiet and contemplative, American raku pottery is big, bold, and eye-catching. Exactly when or how "postfiring reduction" was invented is open to debate, but to most modern American potters the practice of placing pots hot

from the kiln into a barrel of combustible material is the essence of raku. Perhaps it was an accidental discovery, but it may have also been inspired by the Pueblo Indian technique of producing blackened pots by smothering the fire. It is the direct contact of pots with combustible material, integral to both American-style raku and to Native American firing methods, that is at the heart of pit and saggar firing as well. Thus, pit firing is a uniquely American firing process born from the union of raku with Native American firing techniques.

Here, the pottery and firing techniques of Native American potters are described, followed by an overview of Hal Riegger's exploration of raku and pit firing. As he describes his own journey of discovery into raku

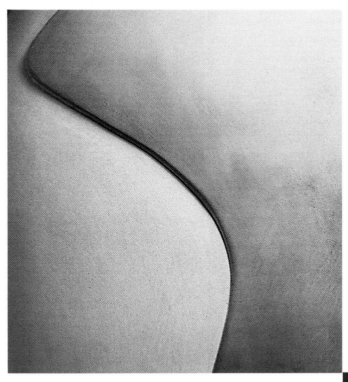

and "primitive" firing, we begin to see the birth of the broad continuum of firing techniques loosely termed pit and saggar firing.

Finding Oaxaca

by Eric Mindling

East Valley Zapotec potters tumblestack pots for a bonfiring; already fired pots and shards are used to insulate the stack.

As the wood settles during the firing, it is repositioned with a long agave stalk to prevent cold spots.

I went far into the south of Mexico to learn some Spanish and see if there was any truth to a couple of black-and-white photos I'd seen in an old book on Mexican pottery. One showed a potter sitting out in the open, making a fine round pot, apparently without a wheel. The other showed a stack of pots enveloped by the leaping flames of a brush and branch bonfire. Through the flames could be seen the sweaty face of the potter as she threw more fuel to the fire. The caption claimed the place to be Oaxaca (pronounced wha ha' ka).

I'd gazed at these photos long and hard through a rainy north coast winter, imagining a place far beyond the overflowing slop buckets and premixed glazes of the university ceramics studio. I envisioned a hard-edged and wide-awake existence in the world of that potter. Was there a place like this, where simple pottery was still being made, where branches and brush were all that were needed to fire a pot? And what kind of potter could make a symmetrical pot without a wheel?

Traveling 70 bus hours south of the small town where I was living put me deep into this other world, and arriving in the city of Oaxaca was like awakening to a dream. All the colors were strong, bright and clear. My eyes, so accustomed to gray Pacific drizzle, burned with the brilliance. I walked down stone streets closed in by yard-thick walls of 500-year-old adobe houses, their cool interior courtyards filled with banana and jasmine. (In the Pacific Northwest, the historic buildings dated to the late 1800s, their walls made of termite-infested wood.) Beyond those heavy low buildings I could see a mountain whose top had been leveled 2000 years ago to build the greatest of the Zapotec cities. The stepped pyramids defined the horizon.

I was told that pottery was being made in two nearby villages, Atzompa and Coyotepec. The potters of Atzompa produced so much functional ware that the work could be found in just about every kitchen in the state. Coyotepec was known for its beautifully burnished, jet black reduction ware. Visiting both of these villages in my first weeks in Oaxaca deeply moved me. I felt as though I could spend the rest of my life learning pottery in either place. But when I looked again at photocopies of those old photos, I could see that they had been taken elsewhere.

Atzompa and Coyotepec were filled with stone and adobe kilns, the houses close together, the comfortable civilization of the city was just minutes away. In the photo, the potter was firing right on the ground; beyond, there was nothing but open, mountainous country. It looked to be a place far removed from city life; it looked like a place where one's comfort came from the light of the sun and where the only avenues were those defined by the walls of the

hills. It was those potters and that place that I'd come here to find.

Ask as I might, no one in the city could tell me anything more about pottery than what I'd already been told. Back home, I'd searched libraries for information on Oaxacan pottery, but there was nothing. So I decided to see for myself what was in those pyramid-capped mountains, heading out past the last stoplight to where the pavement ends and beyond. Before me was the state of Oaxaca, an immense area so varied and remote as to seem to be an entire country in itself.

I found a jumbled terrain with mountains and valleys, ridges and rivers, varying from high thorny deserts to

low green jungle, with but a few decaying roads. The land was lined with arroyos and donkey trails, and generously peppered with pueblos and tiny ranchos, gatherings of adobe houses surrounded by cornfields, and marked in the center by a white-washed stone church. These were backcountry villages, born along arroyos amid the scant flats, where the soil would hold a crop. And there were potters. Hundreds upon hundreds of potters, living in villages throughout the land, with each village keeping a large region well supplied.

Since that first trip into the dirt-road country of Oaxaca, I've spent years on dusty tracks, and have come across dozens of other pottery villages. To me, it is

Strainer pot, 10 inches in height, handbuilt, slipped and roughly burnished, tumblestacked and bonfired, Nahuatl, Guerrero.

The Roots of Pit Firing

Water jug, 16 inches in height, slipped and roughly burnished, tumblestacked and bonfired with wood for about an hour, Nuhuatl Highland, Guerrero.

like finding El Dorado or Shangri-La. Each of these villages will have its own way of forming, of firing, of giving shape to a pot or jug, but all have one thing in common—they are all dedicated to the production of functional pottery. They make the bean and tamale pots, water jugs, cisterns, strainers, spoons, canteens, barrels, bowls and mugs—all the simple, straightforward vessels that keep civilizations watered and fed.

Their work has been an essential part of the Oaxacan backcountry for 4000 years. This is the pottery learned from their mothers, who in turn were taught by their mothers, and so on for 200 generations. They continue to dig their clay from the same old spots, sift sand down by the creek, form round pots on a stone, slipping, burnishing and firing on the ground under a bright blue sky.

To my amazement, I found that the great variety in types of pottery from village to village and region to region was also reflected in the people, or vice versa. Mexico, when it was christened with that name some 500 years ago by the conquering Spanish, was a vast mosaic of nations, peoples and ethnicities. Uniting the land under one name did not cause those nations and peoples to evaporate into history; beyond the cities and the fanfare of the 20th century, they still live on. The potters of Oaxaca are Zapotec, Mixtec, Ayu'uk, Nahuatl. In all, there are 15 languages spoken in Oaxaca and 5 times as many dialects. Indeed, I've often found my hard-learned Spanish of little use. On the other hand, I'm proud to say that I can say "pot" in 7 languages.

And what of the pottery itself? How does one make a symmetrical, round pot without a wheel? After many good hours spent with potters in the shade of a porch or under a tree in the courtyard, I've found the secret. Technically, it goes like this. A lump of clay, perhaps 2 pounds, perhaps 10, is formed into a cone. The point of this cone is then set onto a small piece of leather, a thin flat stone or a scrap of old soccer ball. This is then placed on the floor or a thick slab of stone with a handful of sand tossed beneath. This bit of sand acts as ball bearings upon which the piece of

A scrap from a soccer ball nested in a depression in a large stone allows the pot to turn as Zapotec potter Alberta Mateo Cruz completes its shaping.

Cooking pot, 15 inches in height, slipped three times, burnished twice, tumblestacked and bonfired with wood, San Marcos, Oaxaca.

scrap material, together with the cone of clay, will rotate.

Working seated on the ground, the potter will rotate the cone as she uses her fist and forefinger, then corncobs and a gourd piece to open, push, pull, compress and stretch the clay into a cylinder. If she needs to build up the pot more, she will form coils, and quickly smear and squeeze them onto the rim, using the gourd and corncob to thin and lift the clay. When the pot is well defined, the point of the cone upon which it is formed is trimmed off with a quick slice of a blade, and the base is scraped round.

One can watch a potter peacefully build a 3-foot-tall cylinder, shape, smooth and remove the pot, then go on to the next, all the while chatting away. The whole process looks wonderfully

simple and pleasing. And it is. But from muddy experience, I can attest that making the point of that cone rotate nicely and have anything resembling symmetry happen between your hands and the clay is anything but simple. So, while a clay cone, corncob roller and coiling might provide the technical explanation of how these wonderfully round pots (so light they almost seem to float when one lifts them) are made, they tell an empty story. There is much more to the tale.

Perhaps the most important element in the whole process is the potter's understanding of her materials. She digs her own clay, soaks and sieves it. She sifts in grog, mixing clay bodies by feel and taste, with adjustments for bowls, pots or platters. She makes her tools from gourds, leather, corncobs, old bat-

tery cores, discarded felt hats, metal banding, sardine cans, cactus spines, broken buckets and just about anything else that works. For firing, she gathers wood in the hills with burro and machete, dries cow manure in the sun, collects waste from the agave fields, travels to the lumber mills for scrap, even chops up bug-eaten roof beams. She knows personally and perfectly everything that will go into a pot and how it will behave from forming to firing.

This thorough knowledge of materials is backed by practice. A potter is born into her trade, born into a family that has been making pots for perhaps a dozen generations, perhaps a hundred. She'll start seriously making pots in her adolescence; from then on, clay will be central to her life, until her hands are no longer capable of working. She may

The Roots of Pit Firing

Librada Jose Bautista forms a pot on a large stone; a smaller stone disk at the base of the pot allows it to turn as she works.

harvest, etc. Throughout all this, the pottery work remains constant and sure. Her clay is beneath her feet, her tools are whatever's at hand, and her teacher lives under the same roof.

The pottery of Oaxaca has survived four millennia because it fulfills certain basic needs, such as carrying water and cooking food. Time has taught the potters to fit their forms to these needs. Water jugs are built with small mouths to contain splashing, but with wide bodies to hold volume. In regions where water must be drawn from deep wells, the jugs are ingeniously made with long, bluntly pointed bases and broad shoulders, which cause them to lean over and fill when hitting the water, righting again when full.

Cooking pots are made with a rounded bottom, which helps the pot settle in among the coals and uniformly conduct the heat up the sides of the pot. This same roundness serves another important structural role. As this is very low-fired pottery, it is quite fragile. Most Oaxacan pots follow the lines of a sphere, the strongest form in nature. Also in the name of strength, a great deal of compressing and burnishing of the clay goes into the forming of the pot.

To these potters, the shape is primary. Decoration and finishes are more an afterthought. But what a wonderful afterthought they are! The Zapotec potters of the Southern Sierra paint their pots with a tannin dye made by boiling oak bark. This is splashed onto the pot, using a heavily twigged branch just as the pot is pulled from the hot coals of the firing. It gives the pot the look of ancient, tarnished bronze. These potters claim they dye their pots because the belief in the territory holds that the darker the pot, the better fired it is.

Many hours distant, in the barren Upper Mixteca, the potters of Tonaltepec use the same technique, but their pots are splattered, using oak-dye-soaked rags. The look is wild and modern, yet the best reason that I've heard for this bold finish is "that's how my grandmother did it."

The East Valley Zapotec potters of San Marcos slip their pots up to three

make 50,000 pots in her lifetime. When she is in her mid-twenties, she will be extremely adept at making those pots. By her mid-thirties, she will be able to make pots with her eyes closed. Coming into her fifties, it will seem as though she will simply have to look at the clay for the pots to be made.

I don't mean to imply that the potters here are production machines. They aren't; their work is slow and even paced, and their days and weeks are spent not only making pottery, but also raising children, cooking meals, going to the market, celebrating Easter and Day of the Dead, spending a month with the times with a fine red clay. They are then thoroughly burnished until the pots shine like river-washed stones.

In the Sierra Madre, the potters of Tamazulapan scrape their pots with a corncob. This isn't done for decoration, but simply because corncobs are handy tools there. As a result, their pots have wonderfully rough, textured and furrowed surfaces.

In many villages, aside from the gracefulness of the pot form itself, no decorating is done, except for that which happens in the path of the flames.

Which brings me to that all-powerful moment in a potter's life—firing. This is the way it's done in Oaxaca: A week or two of slow, careful, patient work is set in the sun to warm one morning. By the afternoon, the pots are made firm or made shard by bonfires similar to the one I'd seen in that photo. It is low-fired, single-fired, quick-fired pottery—fired just enough for the life it will lead.

The pots are tumblestacked into a low mound over a bed of wood. This mound is covered over with more wood, then coals from the kitchen are added to start the fire. A bonfiring usually lasts under an hour, with wood or brush added here and there as the potter sees fit. Somewhere in that sweaty hour the smoke changes color, the soot lifts, the pots glow a dull red. The potter knows her work is done. A pyrometer would tell us that this happens at about 1300°F.

At most, such firings consume five or six armloads of fuel. This is an important detail in an arid land where wood must be used not only for firing pots, but for cooking every meal. Its conservation is a must. Had it been necessary to fire this pottery with more wood for all these centuries, it is quite possible that neither the pottery nor these cultures would have survived. No wood, no pots, no cooking fires, no dinner, no people.

The pottery that emerges from such a firing is light and resilient, ideally suited to its purpose. On a cold mountain morning, a pot can be set straight into the flames of the cooking fire with nothing more than a sigh. The sudden heat is simply absorbed and spread through-

out the porous clay. Or when filled with water and left to sit, the pot "sweats" as the water soaks through the open clay. Evaporation of the moisture on the surface cools the water inside, making for a fine way to store drinking water where there is no refrigeration. Sweating pottery and resilience through extreme temperature variation are results of clay bodies that are more than 50% grog and the quick-firing process, which leaves the clay more like sand than glass.

There is a polished coarseness in this quick-fired pottery that I find exhilarating. The roaring flames, smoke, pitch and ash have their way with the surfaces. There is little control to be had, and no pot escapes the branding of the fire.

This wild firing, along with the evolved functionality of the pottery, has redefined what beauty in clay is for me. And the pottery offers a fine reflection of the people who create it. They too are finely coarse and wonderfully rough. They too are pleasingly straightforward, frank in their ways and not distracted by ruffle and finery.

Since that first bright-eyed day in Oaxaca, I have spent years exploring the backcountry, and continue to do so. I have yet to find the potter in that old photo. Truth be told, though, I stopped looking long ago. It wasn't a certain potter that I'd come to find; rather, it was a way of being and doing that I'd longed to find. And that I achieved, not after years of searching, but from the moment I ventured beyond the fast hum of the city and stumbled across a small hidden town filled with potters working hard for a pot of beans. ▲

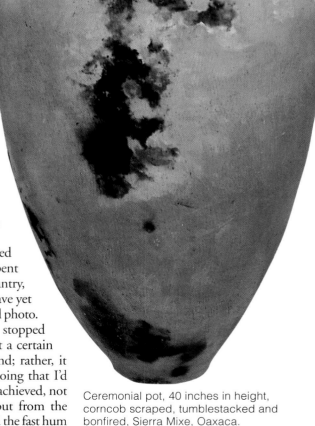

Ceremonial pot, 40 inches in height, corncob scraped, tumblestacked and bonfired, Sierra Mixe, Oaxaca.

The Roots of Pit Firing

All that Glitters

Micaceous Clay

by Constance Shunk

Handbuilt micaceous earthenware bowl with carved and punched decoration, 14 inches in diameter, by Constance Shunk, Los Alamos, New Mexico.

The potential of micaceous clay can best be described as the most widely known secret in the clay world. For centuries, Native American potters from the Taos and Picuris pueblos in New Mexico, as well as some Jicarilla Apache and Navajo potters, have made excellent use of the glittering beauty and versatility of this clay. The high percentage of mica, sometimes as much as 60% mica to 40% clay, gives their pots the appearance of being infused with gold. Collectors, historians, and museum personnel have also been in on the secret, but many contemporary potters and potential buyers have not yet discovered the joy of working with or owning pottery made of micaceous clay.

In the north-central mountains of New Mexico, where Taos and Picuris pueblos are located, pegmatite deposits have served as commercial sources of mica since the 17th century. The Harding pegmatite belt, which covers approximately 60 square miles, stretches from the northwest to the southeast across the northern part of New Mexico's Rio Grande Valley. By the late 1950s, however, mica mining had lost its momentum due to the development of new technologies, particularly in the electronics industry.

Even though much of the mica-mining industry is now defunct, the hillsides and stream beds reflect the abundance of micaceous clay. Other minerals found in this area range from the rare and exotic to the plentiful; among them are lithium, spodumene, fluorite, lepidolite, magnetite, and rutile.

Typically, the raw clay is blunged into a thick slurry, then strained through wire mesh onto a piece of cloth or a plaster bat. Regular window screening is preferred since it will not filter out the larger pieces of mica, but will remove twigs, leaves and other large organic particles. This particular clay seems to require less aging time than other clay bodies, so as soon as the correct amount of moisture has evaporated, it is ready for use.

While Native American potters from other parts of the Southwest must add ground shards to their local clays as temper to help it withstand thermal shock (much as sand or grog is added to raku clay), New Mexico's micaceous clay is naturally tempered and needs nothing adding but water.

When it's thrown on the potter's wheel, the silky feel of micaceous clay makes it slip through the fingers like satin. However, as with an ice cream cone on a hot day, it is over too soon. No wonder the extended pleasure of the handbuilding experience is preferred by some local potters. When asked why, their usual response is that it is like reading a good book—it has to be savored to get the most pleasure from the experience.

Whether it is coiled or slab built, shaping, smoothing and drying are only the preliminaries to a finished piece. After the vessel or sculpture is totally dry, the sanding process begins. Although sandpaper may be used, small pieces (about the size of a fist) of semisoft sandstone make the best tools for smoothing the inside and outside surfaces. There is an interesting interaction between the sandstone and the vessel. As the potter rubs the sandstone over the dry clay, the walls become more uniform. At the same time, the sandstone accommodates itself to the curve of the vessel wall.

After sanding, the pot is ready to be burnished. A slip, about the consistency of thick cream and saturated with mica, is applied with a small cellulose sponge. Several applications of slip are made, then the still-damp pot is burnished with one or more stones chosen for their various surfaces (concave, convex or flat). These polishing stones are treasured and cared for, as is any good pottery tool. Many Native American potters are wise enough to pass these down from generation to generation.

The burnishing process seems to push any grainy or irregular bits of clay into the surface, making it even smoother. Burnishing also removes a thin layer of clay from mica on the

"Hanging Shield with Willow Twigs," 12 inches in diameter, unglazed micaceous earthenware, handbuilt, dried, sanded, slip coated, burnished, and low fired.

surface, making it more visible and light reflective.

After burnishing, the pot is again allowed to dry. By this time, it has taken on the sparkling quality of gold because of the particles of mica in both the clay body and slip applied to the surface. This is the definitive appearance for which micaceous pottery is recognized.

Before the firing, some potters who work with micaceous clay add another step which consists of rubbing the vessel with regular household cooking oil, then slowly heating it in an oven to about 500°F—starting at 150° and slowly increasing by 25° increments. The oil is burned enough to turn the surface completely black. This process seems to cement the flecks of mica to the surface until a kiln or pit firing is completed. The blackened oil is burned off in the final firing, producing a warm, orange color that needs no glazing; however, glazes, washes, or engobes will adhere to the clay.

Pit firing with dung or wood often leaves blackened streaks on the exposed surfaces. Called "fire clouds," these carbon deposits are greatly admired as a vi-

sual reminder of the process of combining clay, water, air and fire—all gifts of Mother Earth.

Total reduction may also be achieved by covering the pit with dirt at the end of the firing process or immediately after firing by placing the pot in a reduction chamber. This chamber may be anything that can be made airtight and is relative to the size of the pot. Any combustible fuel may be used—newspaper, straw, etc.

Other potters, particularly those who add brushed designs, prefer electric kiln oxidation firing. They say the "fire clouds" detract from the overall effect by making the design too complex.

Because New Mexico micaceous clay is an earthenware, the usual firing temperature is very low—from Cone 018 to 015. Though not vitrified at these temperatures, it still is usable as cookware and serving bowls. When the clay is fired to higher temperatures, it does become vitrified; however, the color is brassy and not as pleasing. It has been shown to hold up to temperatures between Cone 010 and 06, but beyond this it begins to slump.

Since mica can be found in many parts of the United States, it is possible to locate mica-saturated clay deposits elsewhere. However, rather than prospecting for natural clays, a potter can add mica or mica flour to any favorite clay body, usually without altering firing temperatures, although some experimentation would be wise. ▲

The Roots of Pit Firing

Tammy Garcia

by Gail Molnar Pfeifer

Twenty-seven-year-old ceramist Tammy Garcia stands poised between two worlds: traditional Santa Clara pottery and contemporary ceramic art. Two years ago at the Santa Fe Indian Market, she won first-place awards in both categories, and her pots sold out in 15 minutes.

Garcia began studying pottery 11 years ago, after leaving high school. "I never intended to make it my career," she admits, but her environment had a powerful influence. Both her mother, Linda Cain, and grandmother, Mary Cain, are well-known potters from Santa Clara Pueblo. And whenever Tammy wants to, she can see pottery made by her great-great-grandmother, Serafina Tafoya, at the Museum of Indian Arts and Culture in Santa Fe.

"I come from four generations of potters," Garcia explains, tracing a finger over the genealogy chart in Rick Dillingham's book *Fourteen Families in Pueblo Pottery,* "so it was a natural thing to try. I started at 16, and for about 3 years studied making pots with my mother. I worked on how to build them, paint them with colored clays, polish, carve and fire them."

After mastering classic Santa Clara red- and blackware, she decided to do more, to express ideas through a more personal style. "I get my ideas from everywhere. I like to go to museums and study ancient Mimbres pots," Garcia explains. But she doesn't try to duplicate them; instead, she absorbs their meaning to generate ideas for her own work. "Two people can have the same idea, but it will look different in the way we express it," she says.

Contemporary art, particularly that of painter Helen Hardin, also influences Garcia's style. "Her work is so geometric," Garcia says, "and I find I can apply that to my pottery design.

Working with clay dug near Santa Clara Pueblo, Tammy Garcia coil builds both traditional and contemporary forms.

"Do you want to see some things I'm working on?" she asks, removing the plastic covering from vessels in various stages of completion. One coil-built piece, about 18 inches high and almost 2 feet in diameter, is still in progress. "These larger ones can take three months to complete," she notes.

"Here's a good example of what I'm doing now," she says, picking up a vessel with crisply drawn dancers. Garcia puts the pot down and flips through a nearby photo album, locating a picture of a Santa Clara Pueblo dancer, arrayed in traditional dress.

"Here is a complex costume my cousin wears for our rain dance, with symbols all over it. I've taken the tablita for example, and drawn it with only two

Each coil is attached by pinching, then smoothed with the fingertips.

bands, to imply a rainbow. The headdress is full of feathers, but I draw just two to suggest them on the pot."

The dancers circle the pot in poses reminiscent of the photograph, and evocative of Helen Hardin's "Corn Dancers" (1968). While evidence of these outside influences is identifiable, Garcia's design is her own, with a carving style that results in images so well defined that they appear laser cut.

What about the controversy over traditional firing methods versus the use of electric kilns in the creation of Native American pottery? Garcia pauses before replying. "I don't like anything to limit my creativity," she says. "I decided I will fire the very large red pieces in an electric kiln, because I can't bear to lose them. A lot of work, time and feeling go into what I do, and I needed that piece to survive in order to make it worthwhile.

"Firing is a mechanical process, anyway," Garcia continues, but she concedes there is skill and knowledge involved in the process of outside firings, which she still does to obtain her classic blackware.

In any discussion of new methods to produce pueblo-style pottery, it's important to remember that the art has

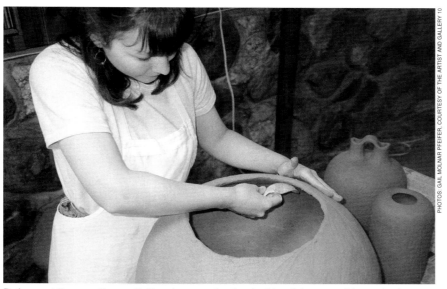

PHOTOS: GAIL MOLNAR PFEIFER, COURTESY OF THE ARTIST AND GALLERY 10

Before adding another coil, Garcia smooths the inside of the pot with a gourd.

always been influenced by market pressures, and by creative people looking for the best ways to produce their work. Contemporary potters might smooth their pieces with sandpaper rather than corncobs, or decorate with hardware-store brushes instead of yucca leaves, but the quality of art produced is, without question, developing in response to buyer demand. This, in itself, is a traditional process. Pueblo potters have always traded their distinctively styled wares among their own tribes, then with

Anglos as trade developed along the Santa Fe Trail.

The issue of honesty about method is at least as important as technique. Indian Market allows potters to submit work in either contemporary (kiln fired) or traditional (outside fired) categories, supporting a great variety of expression in this long underappreciated art form. As time moves forward, potters like Tammy Garcia erase the lines, if they ever really existed, between traditional and contemporary. ▲

A sample of Garcia's smoothing, carving and burnishing tools (old and new) surrounding three chunks of raw clay used to make slip.

Traditional blackware is fired outside in the open.

Carved jar, 16 inches in height, handbuilt and burnished earthenware,
Best of Pottery award winner at the 1995 Indian Market in Santa Fe.

"Pueblo Girls," 19 inches in height, first place (nontraditional category) at the Sante Fe Indian Market.

Blackware jar, 8 inches in height, by Tammy Garcia, Taos, New Mexico.

The Roots of Pit Firing

Raku Then and Now

by Hal Riegger

In the spring of 1948, I thought it would be fun to invite a few friends over, have a potluck supper outdoors and try this raku thing. Aside from Bernard Leach's description and drawings of raku kilns and pots in *A Potter's Book,* the only mention of raku I might have seen was in *The American Ceramic Society Bulletin's* February 1943 issue. At the beginning of Warren Gilbertson's report on "Making of Raku Ware and Its Value in the Teaching of Beginners' Pottery in America," he mentions (almost casually) that raku's major use in the Orient was for the tea ceremony. If either of these sources was where I first heard about raku, I cannot remember. Regardless, I certainly didn't read carefully, or forgot some of what I read.

The weather was perfect for that first raku firing. I lived in the country, partway up Mt. Tamalpais in Marin County, just north of San Francisco. Each of my guests made a couple of teabowls, and while they were drying, we had a fine supper with good California wine, then got down to the business of finishing the bowls. They were glazed raw, then dried again. I'd made a small electric kiln and put it outdoors. I don't remember if I was first or if one of the guests took the initiative, but a bowl was put into the red-hot kiln and the lid replaced. In about a minute, there was a muffled sort of "poof" sound. We knew what had happened.

I turned off the kiln, and cleaned it out with the vacuum cleaner. A second

American raku pioneer Hal Riegger removing a plate from the kiln for postfiring reduction.

pot was then put into the kiln, which had by then been turned on but was not yet red hot. It took about three minutes before that telltale muffled "poof" again.

"Well, that's it!" I thought. "Those Japanese don't know what they're talking about. The heck with raku."

But I didn't want to give up. Alone, over breakfast the next morning, I re-read Gilbertson's article, and there on the very first page, he clearly describes the "biscuit" firing. Maybe the Japanese were okay after all.

More slowly, more carefully, I gave it another try, this time using several little bisqued bowls. Although I had wished for someone to share my excitement, I was alone with my first success: a pinched teabowl, foot turned on the wheel; the glaze was a pale turquoise

with a pink glow inside, and the foot was black.

Before I had an opportunity to do much more raku, a change in jobs took me to Kansas as a designer for a small pottery manufacturer; on return to California, I taught at the College of Arts and Crafts in Oakland. But in 1958, the first time I taught at Haystack, raku was the subject. Those weeks marked the beginning of my serious involvement with the process.

Two years earlier, at the first American Craftsman's Council convention at Asilomar, near Carmel, California, I had met a Japanese potter who had done raku. Of course I quizzed him about all the aspects of raku that I wanted to know. I remember him making a crude little sketch of a raku kiln on a tiny yellow piece of paper. I wish I still had that sketch. Although we didn't follow it exactly, it formed the basis of the kiln we used at Haystack.

During three years of teaching in Florida, from 1958 through 1961, I did some more raku and primitive firings (what people now call "pit" firing). A year after returning from Florida to California, I started what I called Experiment A workshops (the title has absolutely no meaning whatsoever). These were week-long workshops "in the field," where we would find our clay, make and fire pots, all in a very primitive environment. Some of these workshops also dealt with raku fired in wood-burning kilns.

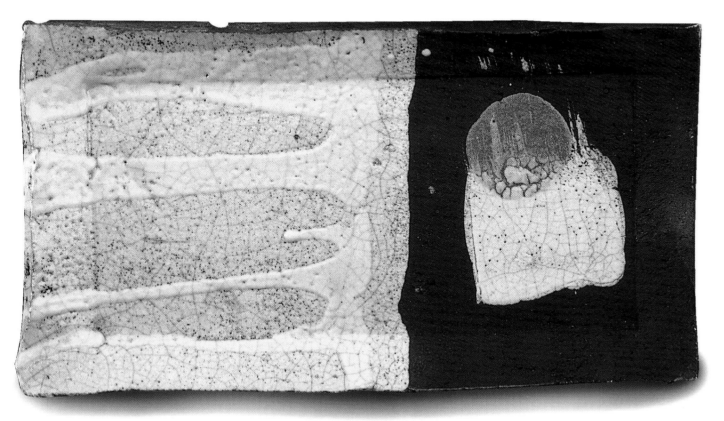

Raku plate, approximately 9 inches in length, with poured and brushed glaze decoration.

Pinched teabowl, approximately 4 inches in height, raku fired.

Raku teabowl, approximately 4 inches in height, pinched, partially brushed with glaze.

The Roots of Pit Firing

A wood-fired raku kiln built from a mixture of fireclay, sandy gravel and sawdust at a British Columbia workshop.

These workshops were held over a period of 17 years in various places around the country, such as the beach at Mendocino, Panamint Valley in the Mojave area, a ghost town in Wyoming and at Cripple Creek in Colorado. Attendees for the primitive pottery workshops were allowed to bring only a shovel and bucket. Other tools had to be found objects. (See "Pottery Making—Indian Style" in the May 1963 CM.)

At first it was hard for us to get away totally from the studio when it came to kilns. Here, we used firebrick and shelves, until one occasion when none were available; it was then that a real breakthrough occurred. An entire wood-burning, top-loading kiln was made from a mixture of clay, sandy gravel and sawdust in more or less equal proportions. We also discovered that a fire could be lit in the wet kiln to dry it out and the mixture wouldn't explode. Although slower than subsequent firings, the first firing took place the day after the clay/gravel/sawdust kiln was built.

Some of the kilns the students built became almost human sculptures with breasts and buttocks.

At any rate, by 1964, we had moved a step further from the limiting influence of studio equipment and routine processes into situations demanding creative thought and inventiveness arising from the situation. And, for raku, this was all to the good. (See my three-part article on raku in the September, October and November 1965 issues of CM.)

As any potter is wont, when presented with a new tool, material or technique, the workshop participants would go all out and try all possible variations. In retrospect, some of the objects produced may not be quite appropriate in the traditional raku context, but we did explore and we did have fun.

I'm at a loss to explain why or even when I did it myself, but one of the things not traditional among raku potters in Japan that is common among Western potters is a technique called "postfiring reduction." In other words,

the pot is put into a reducing atmosphere as it comes out of the glaze firing. This is usually done by placing the pot(s) hot from the kiln into easily combustible materials in a garbage can and covering with the lid.

Somewhere along the line, I chose a different way that I like better: A small amount of sawdust is sprinkled on the ground to receive the hot raku object. A flat object (a plate perhaps) is just laid on the sawdust, and after a short interval, more sawdust is sprinkled on top of it. If rakuing a hollow form, such as a teabowl, I wave it in the air a few seconds, place it on the sawdust and push sawdust up to the rim on the outside only. After perhaps a minute, more sawdust is sprinkled on, burying the whole object. This wait is necessary, as the inside glaze cools more slowly and must solidify or sawdust will mar its surface.

Western postreduction techniques may well have arisen from a misunderstanding of the traditional Japanese reduction, which was done after the bisque and before glazing. Usually made of a very rough white clay, the bisque-fired teabowls were brushed with ocher, then placed in a fireclay box along with charcoal, which was then ignited. The whole process is a bit more detailed than what I have written here, but is well described and illustrated in Herb Sanders' book *The World of Japanese Ceramics.*

After I quit having the workshops, I began to look at where I was with raku, what I was doing, how integral the process was to the result. In other words, were the things I was doing possible only with the raku process, or could they be made using any of a number of other methods available to potters?

To me, this is the key. It's not a matter of what materials one works with, what temperature one works at, or whether the firing is done with electric-ity, gas or wood, but whether the object is one that could only be made with the raku process.

If I wanted to go further, following the more traditional ways that tie in with Zen philosophy, I could ask of this work whether it has the qualities that are so important to adherents of the tea ceremony. While most raku potters in America do not assess their pots in the same manner as a Japanese Zen master, there are aspects of a good ceremonial teabowl that can apply and are indeed valuable for the Western potter to understand and assimilate.

The traditional raku teabowl is handmade from a rough, gritty clay, yet when completed, is pleasant to the touch. A summer teabowl is shallow and wide, while a winter teabowl is taller and narrower. For its size, it is thick but not heavy. It is asymmetrical; the rim undulates. There is a front and a back. The base rim (foot) must be so shaped that the bowl is easily picked up by the thumb and two fingers. The bottom inside must have a depression called a *cha damari,* or tea pool, where the last few drops of tea will look like rain collecting in a depressed rock (the potter consciously puts the cha damari there, yet it is supposed to look like it just sort of happened). The bowl must be larger at the lower belly to allow room for the whisk. And, finally, the inside must appear larger than the outside!

Once, when discussing these aspects with a Japanese raku potter, I remarked, "You know, is this rationalizing? I wonder if this isn't all a lot of hog wash."

To which he replied, "Now you're getting into Zen." ▲

Raku plate, approximately 9 inches in length, sandy red clay, with clear glaze, borax solution and trailed white glaze, by Hal Riegger, Gridley, California.

PIT FIRING:
A unique American firing technique

Whether a pit firing is a solitary or social event depends on the size of the pit. Assuming the pit is to be dug in soft soil—frequently in sand at a beach—it can be large enough for several dozen pots. Thus pit firing is eminently suitable for workshops or classes. The basic process begins with digging a pit, usually no more than 3 or 4 feet wide and 18 inches to 24 inches deep, but as long as necessary. The bottom is covered with a layer of sawdust into which bisqued pots are nestled. Materials such as copper carbonate and salt can be sprinkled in to add yellow and red flashing. A pit dug in beach sand may well benefit from the saltiness of the sand itself— and at one particular beach where the sand is so full of black bits of iron that a magnet dropped in the sand comes up looking furry, pots emerge from the pit with extra orange flashing. After the pots are arranged in the pit they are covered with kindling and firewood, and set alight.

The pit can be covered with sheet metal to retard the fire and promote reduction coloring; it may or may not be restoked before being allowed to burn out. The variations in results come from the length of the firing and the fuel used, whether sawdust or wood shavings, hard or soft wood, or dung; the materials added, which can include seaweed, other organic materials, or copper scrubbing pads; the arrangement of pots either loosely or tightly, in a single layer or stacked; and of course the type of clay used, whether it is burnished or not, and the temperature of the bisque firing. Upon unloading, the pots will be rich black wherever they touched the sawdust, with red, orange and yellow flashing from copper and salt. The pots may be cleaned if necessary, and waxed to protect and enhance the surface.

The articles that follow describe four variations on this basic pit-firing method. These four approaches represent a few of the many variations possible with this versatile technique. Through trial-and-error, each of these artists has found ways to make pit firing work for them. Working with different clays and different combustible and volatile materials, each has evolved a personal pit-firing technique.

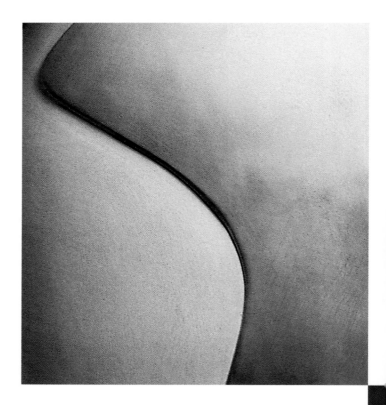

Pit Firing
in North Carolina
by Dan and Linda Riggs

It was probably soon after the discovery of fire that early humans realized that heated clay became harder, more durable. The fact that clay could be imprinted with shapes and colors applied was an aesthetic plus. Today, the ancient technique of pit firing is becoming increasingly popular because of those aesthetic pleasures, although the shapes and surfaces of the pots reveal the modern touch of artistic form, as well as the calculated use of chemicals and just the right amount of sawdust and wood.

Edge Barnes and Zoie Holtzknecht, two potters from the Raleigh-Durham-Chapel Hill area (the "Research Triangle") of North Carolina, are among those who currently are experimenting with pit-firing techniques. Although they come from very different backgrounds, and work in vastly different fields (Holtzknecht in medical transplant research and Barnes in the

PHOTOS: DAN RIGGS

Ovoid vase, 8 inches in height, wheel-thrown stoneware, bisque fired to Cone 09, wrapped with steel wool and copper wire, gas fired to 1500°F in a loose saggar filled with oak chips, copper sulfate crystals, sea salt and seaweed, by Edge Barnes, Raleigh, North Carolina.

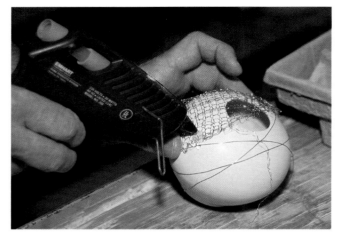

Copper mesh can be held in place with hot glue.

Metal and clay bowls are used as a saggar.

Thin slabs of paper clay will trap fumes near the surface.

Holtzknecht prepares a firing bundle with a mixture of volatiles and combustibles.

Bowl, approximately 8 inches in diameter, wheel-thrown stoneware, pit fired in oak chips, surrounded by copper sulfate, raw cotton and coarse steel wool, by Zoie Holzknecht.

Bottle, 10 inches in height, gas fired to 1500°F in a loose saggar filled with oak chips, copper sulfate, sea salt, seaweed, steel wool and copper wire, by Edge Barnes.

Edge Barnes sprinkling baking soda around a copper-wire-wrapped pot nestled in the sawdust.

Barnes carefully brushing aside ash and debris to remove the fired ware from the pit.

furniture industry), they share a passion for surface markings achieved by placing their bisque-fired pots, along with various chemicals and organic materials, in a sawdust- and wood-filled pit.

Barnes generally likes to burnish his leather-hard pots with a stone. This is followed by buffing with plastic or a soft cloth to increase the shine. Holtzknecht, on the other hand, likes a rougher finish and focuses more on developing color on the surfaces of her pots. Flashes of color on pit-fired ware are achieved by intimate contact with volatile materials, such as copper and salt.

For example, Barnes often wraps part of a Chore Boy copper scrub pad around a pot, holding the stretched wire in place with hot glue from a gun. The copper wire can also be covered with slabs of paper clay, which act like a saggar, trapping the vaporizing copper next to the surface.

A more conventional technique involves the addition of copper sulfate to a saggar. Barnes uses a metal bowl for the saggar, adds copper sulfate, then the copper-wire-wrapped pots, peanut shells, cotton balls and rock salt, cover-

ing the arrangement with an inverted ceramic bowl.

Another method involves placing the pot on a large piece of newspaper, wrapping or draping it with steel wool or copper wire, and sprinkling copper sulfate and rock salt over and around it. Combustibles, such as cotton balls, banana peels, dry dog food, dried flowers, etc., are then placed on the newspaper, which is subsequently rolled around the pot. The newspaper holds the sulfate, salt and combustibles in close proximity to the pot's surface, where they will add interesting designs and colors.

Once the pots are ready for the firing, the next step is to prepare the pit. For the firing shown here, Barnes and Holtzknecht used a large pit, dug by a backhoe to a depth of about 16 inches. Some people prefer shallower pits to produce brighter colors; others prefer pits as deep as 4 feet.

Over a loose bed of wood and newspaper, they laid a course of very dry sawdust (4 to 5 inches thick). While the newspaper-wrapped pots and metal-bowl saggars could be nestled right next to one another in the sawdust, the "na-

ked" pots were spaced several inches apart. Copper sulfate, baking soda and rock salt were then sprinkled around the pots. Dry dog or cat food, banana peels and seaweed could also be added.

A 2- to 3-inch-thick layer of sawdust was poured over the pots, then several feet of wood. Barnes prefers to use thin wood strips, as these burn much quicker and hotter than thicker pieces.

The fire was started with a torch in four or five places, so that the combustibles would burn evenly throughout the entire pit. When it had burned down somewhat, another 1- to 2-foot layer of wood was added.

The pit was then left to burn out. The pots were retrieved only when they were cool enough to handle. Removing ware too early can cause cracking.

Pit-fired pots can be cleaned and lightly polished by rubbing with a cloth. For a brighter shine, wax can be applied; Barnes uses Butcher's Wax.

There are probably as many variations in pit-firing technique as there are potters, which makes every piece unique. The thrill of discovery exists each time the cooled ashes are pushed aside. ▲

Pit-fired vessel, approximately 12 inches in diameter, wheel thrown and burnished.

Energy and Care
Pit Firing Burnished Pots on the Beach
by Carol Molly Prier

Upon returning from a first-time trip to New England, a former student talked about seeing miles of stone fences. He found them extremely beautiful and was fascinated by the energy and care it took to gather and place each stone. He felt that all the energy that had been put into these stone fences came out again as he viewed them. I find this to be true of claywork as well—all the energy and care we put into the making of a ceramic object come out again when one views and experiences the object. I think of this often when I burnish pots.

Unlike most American potters, my interest in burnishing clay did not begin with seeing pueblo pottery but with my love of old Eskimo sculpture. It was discovering that I could make clay look and feel like polished bone that led to further experimentation around 1975. My first burnished pieces were poles up

to 9 feet in height; they were made as hollow tubes and assembled over a wooden armature. Eleven poles "demarking space" were assembled as my M.F.A. project at Mills College in Oakland, California, in 1977.

Following graduation, my interest in burnishing and pit firing continued, but after working in landscape scale with my "Magic Poles," I wanted to switch to a more intimate scale. I was also concerned with the old Eskimo concept that "magic" or power comes from handling an object, so I made a series of curved bonelike pieces with tiny bits of loose clay inside. As people lifted these "Mystery Sticks," the kinetic shift of these tiny clay beads and the resulting sound "revealed" the interior space of the object. (Eleven years later, I would see my first rainstick brought up from Central America!)

During those years when I was burnishing and pit firing sculptural pieces, I used what I called the "cheater" method of pit firing. I would preheat the work in a kiln for about two hours, gradually increasing temperature. Meanwhile, I would prepare a bed of hot coals outside in a small brick enclosure, then run back and forth to take the pieces from the kiln and place them in the coals. I would then build up the fire around the work in the "pit."

Two years ago, I had a wonderfully reaffirming opportunity to work with Steve Lucas (Koyemsi) on the Hopi reservation. Steve is Nampeyo's great-great-grandson. He also preheats his pots (in his kitchen oven), and when coals from sheep dung are hot, he dons gloves to carry the pots outside, placing them on shards on a grate above the coals, then builds up the fire.

Handbuilt and burnished vessel, approximately 5 inches in height, pit fired.

Burnished, pit-fired vessel, approximately 8 inches in height.

Early on, I also experimented a lot with colored terra sigillata polished with a soft cloth. Although I was able to obtain some beautiful colors with additions of iron, ocher, burnt sienna, etc., I was never able to achieve as high a polish as when I burnished the clay itself. Burnishing terra sigillata with a stone to gain a higher polish often resulted in flaking or chipping.

Now, I burnish the clay four different times, beginning at leather hard, then letting the clay dry between each burnishing. The last burnish is done when the clay is completely dry; oil is applied and the surface allowed to dry before burnishing with a polished stone.

I made burnished sculptural pieces for about eight years, then around 1983 began making burnished pots, experimenting with wheel throwing the shapes I had seen in books on pueblo pottery. I also experimented with clays that would not only burnish well but also were strong enough to throw the horizontal shoulder so prominent in pueblo pots, and eventually settled on a midrange stoneware with very fine grog.

As I learned to throw these pueblo shapes, I made a conscious decision not to try to recreate Native American painted or carved designs. I wanted to work with the strong pueblo shapes, but make the pieces my own through my method of firing. To have surfaces marked by the movement of the fire is, in intent, almost opposite to the desired results of traditional pueblo firings, where the intent is not to have any of the intricately painted designs obscured by markings made by the fire. Either shards or pieces of metal are placed over the pots to allow only heat, rather than direct flame, to touch the pots, thus protecting the designs from any extraneous "cloud" markings. When I fired with Steve Lucas, we laughed about how my firings were "backward," the dung placed flat against the pots so the flame would mark the surfaces. His pieces were carefully protected by shards.

As I worked on my throwing methods, I also experimented with different ways of pit firing. In my early firings, the pieces were placed either directly on prestarted coals or on a metal grate (with cow dung under the grate and then around the pieces). Now, I nestle each pot in sawdust to obtain an area of solid black that contrasts with the swirls of fire movement.

I also tried adding different oxides (iron, cobalt, nickel, rutile, etc.) to the pit fire to fume the pots with the movement of the flame. Copper carbonate was the only one to give consistent color. Later, after seeing a lovely piece at a show that was labeled "low-fire salt," I added seaweed to the firings. The salt from the seaweed seemed to intensify the colors from copper and to add a range of yellows to orange. (I live and do my firings on the Point Reyes Peninsula, which is one of the most beautiful seashore areas in the world, and seaweed is readily available.)

Each type of clay reacts differently to the fuming. Most white clays will blush pink, but on some the results will be spotty. White clays also don't develop

The pots are placed in a bed of sawdust, along with seaweed and copper carbonate.

Dry cow dung is placed around and over all the pots, followed by a layer of wood (mixed hard- and softwoods).

Once lit, the pit burns with a lot of flame for about 30 minutes, then a quiet flame for a few hours.

Pit Firing

Once the fire has burned down, all that remains of the dung is thick ash.

Pit-fired vessel (same pot as above after cleaning), approximately 12 inches in diameter, by Carol Molly Prier, Point Reyes Station, California.

wood can), and it leaves a thick ash, which protects the pots as they cool. Making it possible for the pots to cool evenly and slowly is as critical to their not cracking as the manner in which they are heated.

My firing method has evolved as the following: At the beach, I dig a pit about 2 feet deep in the sand, then line the bottom with 4–5 inches of sawdust (mixed hard- and softwood is best). The pots are placed in the sawdust in a tight single layer. Whatever area of the piece that is in direct contact with the sawdust will turn black; if the mouth of an upside-down pot is in the sawdust, the inside will turn black. I then sprinkle copper carbonate and place seaweed around each piece. Table salt or rock salt also works.

The dry cow dung is placed around and over all the pots, then a layer of wood is laid on top. I have found that mixed hard- and softwoods of various sizes from fine kindling up to 2×4-size work best. I do not use plywood, particleboard or painted wood because of glues and toxins. Crumpled newspaper tucked in between all the wood acts as the starter fuel.

Once lit, the pit will burn with a lot of flame for about 30 minutes, then a quiet flame for the next few hours. I do not add wood and I do not pull any piece out until I can touch it without gloves. Unlike raku, which usually uses heavily grogged clay for its thermal-shock resistance, the clays I use have either very fine or no grog at all, which accounts for their ability to burnish nicely. The firing, including cooling, takes about four hours from lighting to pulling out the pieces.

Each piece is then washed and rubbed gently with 0000 steel wool to gently remove any residue. I do not scrub heavily, as rough treatment can scratch or chip the burnish. Finally, I apply a tiny bit of paste floor wax to each piece, then buff with a soft cloth.

All the energy of careful hours of making, burnishing and firing are now returned in the experiencing of each piece. I've done half in the making; the fire has met me in the marking: grace and gratitude. ▲

the soft-to-intense oranges as well as tan or darker clay bodies. The darker wine reds are usually seen on the buff tan to darker clays.

Although initially I did not bisque the pots (relying instead on a one- to three-hour preheat in a nearby kiln), I decided to start bisque firing after I began to teach more workshops for a nearby college in San Francisco. For many students, the workshop would be their only clay experience, and loss is a

very difficult teacher. Bisquing at Cone 011–010 leaves a good burnish, but is high enough to give the pots strength.

Having the desire to work very simply (I dislike the idea of carrying large pieces of corrugated metal and grates to the beach) influenced my method of pit firing. Consequently, I fire quickly in a shallow pit that has a lot of air, thus flame, moving through it. For fuel, I use dung, because it burns very hot and evenly (it doesn't suddenly flare up as

Embree De Persiis

Air-regulated Sawdust Firing

by Robert Reese

From her deck, which looks past vivid green clumps of live oaks and redwoods to the spine of the Big Sur mountains and the Pacific Ocean, it is easy to imagine that Embree De Persiis would be preoccupied with tone and color in her claywork. But form is her primary concern.

"I try to zero in on the essentials, and let the objects speak for themselves. To me, the form is the most exciting part. Usually, I start with only an inkling of what I want from the work; this becomes clearer as it goes on. Once finished, I often look at it and think, 'Oh, so that's what I wanted to say!'

"I like the complex interconnection between forms that are basically simple—circles and ovals. For me, they are at the same time strong and sensual," she explained.

A full-time potter for the past 15 years, De Persiis balances her work between pit-fired vessels and dinnerware she sells from her studio and at the Ventana Lodge in Big Sur.

"I still have real trouble doing both types of work at the same time because it's difficult to switch modes. I worked for a month on three nonfunctional pieces that were in the show, while the dinnerware went on hold," she said.

Born in Georgia, De Persiis was raised in Montreal, and earned a B.A. in English at McGill University, before moving to New York City in 1965 to edit trade publications for Harper & Row and W. W. Norton. While in New York, she attended *New Yorker* magazine cover artist Ilonka Karasz's Design Studio, where students were given free rein to pursue an array of artistic disciplines.

"Ilonka's students seemed already successful in some medium—writing, music composition, photography, bookmaking—while I was just beginning to learn about clay," De Persiis recalled.

Through hours of drill at the Design Studio, she learned fundamentals of art from a "theoretical and spiritual" standpoint. "It might take weeks before one could come up with a drawing of a single leaf that would make Ilonka say, 'At last, a leaf.'" Today, scattered among the oak trees below De Persiis's house, are hundreds of shards, vestiges of the perfectionism instilled by Karasz.

From New York, De Persiis moved to Los Angeles, though not before serving an apprenticeship with Elizabeth White, a Hopi potter living in Oraibi, Arizona. This was where she first experienced "a way of making a living that integrated

Nearly covered by passion flower vines, De Persiis' studio overlooks Palo Colorado Canyon in the Big Sur mountains of the California coast.

A full-time potter, Embree De Persiis balances production of both pit-fired vessels and glazed dinnerware.

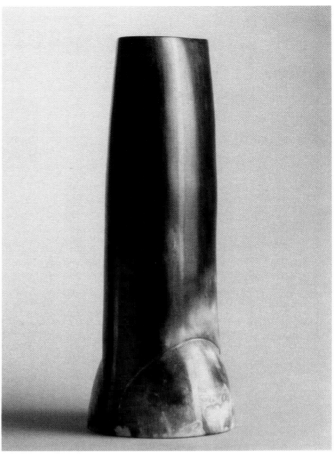

Pit-fired vase, 12 inches high; color was controlled by firing the pot inside a stove pipe drilled with holes.

Porcelain vase, 12 inches in height, bisqued, then pit fired in seaweed and sawdust, by Embree De Persiis.

both the practical and spiritual.

"In Oraibi, I woke up in a house with walls made of clay; we ate from dishes made of clay; we gathered clay from the foot of a mesa. My Indian friend could tell a good sample of clay by its taste, and would cast a sidelong glance at me as she pinched a piece out of a freshly made pot and popped it into her mouth."

Less than two years after De Persiis moved into her Big Sur home/studio, a mud slide cut a swath down the canyon, chopping off the deck and leaving the house on a precipice. Fortunately, her home was saved and the deck rebuilt with the help of neighbors. Today, the yard is terraced and fortified, planted with pine trees and a neat herb garden near the pit where she fires pots.

Even her production coffee mugs and the large glazed dinner plates have something to do, with the precipitous changes that characterize Big Sur. Surfaces and forms are subtly permeated with those impressions: robust wheel-thrown shapes, pure white expanses with slashes

of copper red, cobalt and rutile.

Colors on the pit-fired vessels—splashes of lavender, orange and magenta, iridescent browns, luminous blacks flecked with orange—are the result of altering air flow around burning sawdust and seaweed.

"Controlling air currents in a pit firing is a chancy affair, at best," De Persiis commented. "Open-end stove pipes of varying diameters are slipped over pieces to achieve a variety of effects during a single firing. Holes pierced in their sides regulate air flow—several holes for a whiter surface; fewer for black.

"The pit is partially filled with sawdust, then the pipes are placed on top (some wrapped in seaweed or sprayed with copper) are positioned within the pipes. Additional sawdust is poured to fill the pipes and the remainder of the pit.

"The sawdust is then ignited and, when the fire is burning vigorously, a piece of sheet metal is loosely fitted as a pit cap. Depending on the weather and the number of pieces included,

the firing can take anywhere from 6 to 12 hours; and another 12 hours is allowed for cooling."

De Persiis works daily in a sunny studio that is just off the main house and is nearly covered in passion flower vines. Inside is a small wood-burning stove, oil paintings by friends and neighbors, an ominous-looking electrical device for coloring titanium wire added to some pit-fired pots, plus row after row of functional ware neatly stacked on wooden shelves.

Among the potter's tools that made the journey west with De Persiis is a quote by composer John Cage, nailed next to her wheel: "When you start working, everybody is in your studio—the past, your friends, enemies, the art world and, above all, your own ideas. But as you continue, they start leaving one by one, and you are left completely alone. The, if you're lucky, even you leave." ▲

Smoked and Pit-Fired Porcelain

by Rebecca Urlacher

Working with porcelain has tested my imagination, taxed my creativity and tried my patience. While it is among the most difficult clays to build with, I work with porcelain because of its physical attributes.

As my understanding of the medium grew, I found that the potter's wheel was not allowing the creative expression I was after. Sure, numerous mugs and bowls, all of the same basic size and shape, could be the result of throwing merely a couple hours, but that was not what I wanted to do with porcelain. Working at this expeditious pace was not conducive to creating individual form. Instead, building by hand satisfies my artistic sensibility.

Each piece requires a week or two of attention. To begin, I construct a strong base. If I want a rounded bottom, I pinch a bowl; otherwise, I cut the base from a rolled slab. The wall is then built to about a foot in height by piecing small slabs together. I stop building at this point so the clay has time to dry just enough to be able to support additional pieces.

These forms can exceed 24 inches and require patience and complete focus. During the building process, it is important for me to know the characteristics and physical limitations of the

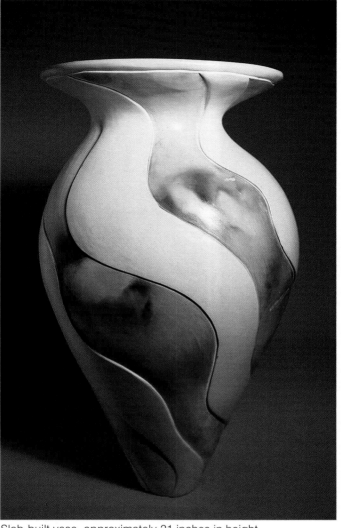

Slab-built vase, approximately 21 inches in height, porcelain, smoked with newspaper.

clay. At the same time, I try not to place restrictions upon myself when I'm deciding how the piece should be shaped. My main objective is to build a form with pleasing lines and curves.

When I think I have pushed the porcelain as far as it will go, I take a step backward to see just what is happening. Because I choose not to use molds or props, it is extremely important for me to look the piece over carefully at this point. Are the sides warping? Is the bottom sagging?

Once the majority of the piece has been built, the challenge is to make sense of the form. How is the opening going to relate? Does it need a lid? Will carved lines add to the liveliness? At times, I am overwhelmed by all the possibilities; however, I like the fact that this approach allows me the flexibility to work without a game plan or blueprint. By far, the most enjoyable aspect of handbuilding with porcelain is this process of discovering new forms. Even when the piece is not successful in the end, I am always able to learn something each time I sit down to build.

The next few days are laborious, as I scrape, sand and sometimes carve the surface. I scrape with a metal rib when the piece is leather hard. Carving is done at the stiff-leather-hard stage. When the form is bone dry, I sand with silicon carbide paper. After the bisque firing, some of these forms are smoked, while others are pit fired.

Smoke firing in a metal can is extremely simple and quick. I start by crumpling some newspapers, then pack them on the bottom and around the sides of the can. Next, I nest the piece in the paper and pack more crumpled newspaper around it. Finally, I light the

Porcelain vase, approximately 20 inches in height, constructed from small slabs, smoked in a metal can filled with newspapers.

Vessel, approximately 15 inches in height, pit-fired porcelain.

Pit-fired vases, to approximately 16 inches in height, handbuilt porcelain, by Rebecca Urlacher, Eugene, Oregon.

Handbuilt porcelain vase, approximately 15 inches in height, fired in a pit filled with charcoal, driftwood, manure, seaweed, copper carbonate and rock salt.

paper and let it burn for approximately two minutes, before pulling the piece from the can (while wearing heat-resistant gloves).

The longer the piece is left in the burning paper, the darker the color. This smoking technique is somewhat controllable and produces subtle shades of brown that contrast nicely with the white of the porcelain.

If I am after a more dramatic effect with a wide range of colors, the piece is pit fired. The size of the pit depends on how many pots are to be fired, but in general the dimensions are 4 feet wide by 6 feet long by 3 feet deep.

After about 20 pounds of charcoal are poured into the pit and lit, I organize all the items that will be going into the pit. Once the charcoal is nearly red hot, it is spread evenly over the bottom of the pit. I then toss in a layer of driftwood (or whatever wood is avail-

able to me at the time), manure, seaweed, copper carbonate and rock salt.

The work is then carefully nested in this layer, followed by more copper, salt and combustibles. I usually heap the pit with sticks, leaves, grass—basically whatever is safe to burn.

Once it starts to smoke steadily, I cover the pit with sheet metal. The fire usually burns overnight, maybe ten hours or so, and the pit can be unloaded in the morning.

During the pit firing, I try to let go of any preconceptions as I anxiously await results. Colors can range from browns and black to shades of orange, red and purple. No two forms ever come out of the fire the same. In a manner of speaking, the fire becomes a collaborator. Occasionally, a bad firing will occur; however, these are outweighed by the unimaginable and stunning results that pit firing can produce. ▲

PIT FIRING BRANCHES OUT:
Pit and sawdust firing in brick chambers and barrels

Potters who engage in pit firing on a regular basis tire quickly of hauling wood, sheets of metal, pots, and other materials to a suitable site for every firing. They begin to want to streamline the process and create a permanent place for firing. Thus, mirroring those prehistoric potters who first began to advance beyond the pit and build structures for containing the fire, modern potters simulate a firing pit with a simple brick box. This can be a permanent structure of mortared bricks, or a temporary one expandable to accommodate a larger or smaller batch of ware. It may be made with solid walls open only on top, or the bricks may be loosely stacked to allow air flow through the walls. Simplifying even further, many potters use a barrel or trash can, usually with nail holes punched in to allow air for combustion.

Standard pit firing is best suited for groups of potters working together to make the firing an exciting, cooperative venture with enough tasks for everybody and success only if all pitch in. A certain amount of insecurity is built in—what if the weather doesn't cooperate or the sand or soil is wet from recent rain? Assuming a suitable site is permanently available, firing in a brick pit removes some of that insecurity and reduces the amount of preliminary labor. With a permanent brick pit, a smaller group of people, with less time to spend preparing the firing site, can carry out a successful firing. Using a small temporary structure or a barrel, potters can indulge in more experimentation, quickly adjusting the size and shape of the brick enclosure to accommodate the work to be fired. The firing itself may be just as protracted as in a standard pit, to encourage color development, or it may be a matter of a few minutes just to create smoke markings.

The greatest difficulty when firing in a small brick chamber, and particularly in a barrel, is in achieving the exciting colors associated with pit firing. A large pit will take many hours to burn out, in the process reaching a relatively high temperature. The high temperature and the flow of air through the pit collaborate to impart spectacular

color to the pots. Three of the artists featured in this chapter are concerned with color development, and have taken different approaches to solving the problem.

The move toward firing in a structure rather than in a pit is one of increasing control over the firing process. Pit firing, while fun, is fraught with variables which can be frustrating for a serious artist. It can be difficult to wait for the right weather when preparing for an exhibition! Clearly, however, no artist wants to sacrifice interesting and beautiful surface effects simply for the increased convenience of firing in a barrel. The artists featured in this chapter illustrate a variety of approaches toward the problem of achieving exciting results when firing in a chamber or barrel.

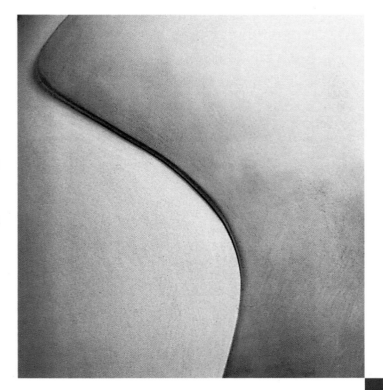

Salt Pit and Sawdust Firing

by Peter Gibbs

Everyone knows somebody who does a bit of pit or sawdust firing. They all use the "best" method and think that everyone else is crazy. The truth is that every culture throughout history up to and including our own has had its own system. And what's more, they're all correct.

I started sawdust firing five or six years ago; but, after tiring of straight black-and-white pots, started pit firing to get more color. The methods described here work particularly well for my pots and my clay, and are a good starting point for anyone interested in experimenting with firing this way.

To begin with, plan on firing simple forms. The surface created in a pit (or sawdust) firing is complex and beautiful enough, without some tricky sort of form to complicate matters. I like to stick with forms based on the sphere because they are simple, strong and easy to handle. Also, if they have necks, the customer can relate to them as familiar bottle forms (no cultural threat attached), and they can get on with appreciating the beauty of the pots without having to grapple with any complex aesthetic questions.

A well-burnished surface will get the most out of these firing processes, so I stick with a fairly fine-grained clay (no particles larger than 80 mesh). A white clay will show off the colors, although other clays will work well too.

Prior to a typical pit firing. I might throw 50 small bottles, say a pound of clay each. Depending on the season, they are covered all night or left exposed. The aim is to be able to start trimming them first thing in the morning.

The pots are trimmed in a freshly thrown clay chuck. On hand are a number of foam rubber disks, slashed through the center, which can be placed in the chuck to prevent the pots from sticking. Generally, the whole pot is trimmed to get the form just right. Because the top will be a little drier, I start there. The pot is placed rightside up in the chuck, trimmed, then burnished at the neck (inside and out) with a teapot piercing tool. If the neck is a bit hard, which it often is, I just hold a damp sponge against it to whip up a bit of slurry on the surface before burnishing. By the time I've worked through a board of ten or so pots, I'm ready to go back to trim and burnish the bottom halves. For the main part of the pot, a thin, stiff rubber kidney does a fast burnishing job, followed by the sidewall of a thin stainless steel rib for a high shine; the back side of a teaspoon may be used on the base. The foam rubber in the chuck should prevent any bruising of the burnished surface.

After bisque firing to about 1650°F (900°C), those bottles are ready to pit fire. At one time I fired in a hole in the ground, but holes in the ground bring all sorts of uncontrollable variables, mainly depending on the weather but also on the type and condition of earth in your area. So a year or two ago, we built a rectangular brick chamber with interior dimensions of 20 inches by 64 inches with a depth of 30 inches. These dimensions are not critical; the only reason for choosing them is that we usually have on hand several tons of wood cut to 32-inch lengths for our large wood-burning kiln. Also, that particular depth allows sufficient coverage of wood so that stoking is unnecessary. The bricks were laid with a fireclay mortar to keep the structure airtight, and there is a light metal frame around the top of the wall to hold it together.

The pots are placed on a bed of 3-4 inches of dry sawdust. We live in a pine forested area and can get a truckload of pine sawdust for next to nothing, so that is what we use. The type of sawdust used may make a difference, but it isn't critical.

Because the part of the pot that is in contact with the sawdust will come out black, some thought should be given to results when putting the ware in the pit. The pots can be placed as close to one another as you like; in fact I think the best results occur when they are close together.

Only one layer of pots is fired at a time. If I have more than that, I just keep firing on consecutive days. But there's nothing to stop you from building a larger pit. We successfully fired one over 20 feet long during a workshop.

For color, I add 1-2 cups each of salt and copper sulfate (bluestone). This should be distributed fairly carefully as too much in contact with the clay will eat into the body and lumps will "spit," resulting in dark spots. I generally scratch around the pots with a stick to make channels between them, then sprinkle the dry, lump-free materials evenly about, dusting off any that land on the ware.

Care should be taken not to breathe any of the materials used for sawdust firing; this includes colorants and the sawdust itself.

Wood is gently piled on top of the pots leaving no room for air to circulate. The wood I use is pine because of convenience. When the pit is completely full, a fire at the top is lit with a bit of newspaper and kindling. As soon as the flame is established, the pit is covered with corrugated iron. The flame will be fairly brisk in the spaces around the edges. I rake out charred wood to fill these spaces as much as possible. Constantly choking off the air supply seems to be one of the most important factors in promoting strong color. Toward the end of the firing, when there are just a few inches of glowing charcoal left, I rake it out evenly, then weight the corrugated iron down with a few bricks. The firing will take from four to six hours, possibly longer.

Mostly the pots will be black from the sawdust, with perhaps a border of white where the carbon burns out in the oxidizing period at the end of the firing. Adjacent to this area will be flashes of red and orange or tan from the copper and salt.

I apply a natural wax to pit-fired pots to give added depth to the surface, and an irresistible sheen for the customer.

Before doing this, each pot must be carefully washed, as dirt picked up while waxing can ruin the surface. The washed ware is generally put into an electric kiln or oven to dry, and to warm it for easier wax application as well.

Although I use salt and copper sulfate in every firing, they are not the only materials which can be added. I am currently experimenting with sulfates of cobalt and iron, neither of which do much just sprinkled into the pit. The best method seems to be applying them to the bisqued pot by dipping, spraying or brushing, then bisquing again. Another color option is to work with stained clay bodies.

Appealing as these pots are, sawdust-fired work, with its strong contrasts of black and white, can be far more dramatic. For this type of firing, I use a similar, but smaller chamber, just stacked loosely with no mortar, and a 3-inch gap between each brick to let in air and encourage white areas.

Having constructed the firing chamber (which may take only five minutes), I pour in 2-3 inches of sawdust, then add alternate layers of pots and sawdust, keeping the pots fairly close together to prevent them from tumbling about as the sawdust burns away. The final layer consists of 3-4 inches of sawdust.

A fire is started at the top. Once the sawdust is smoldering, the chamber is covered with an old piece of corrugated iron and left alone until the sawdust has burned away. The sawdust-fired pots are then washed and waxed in the same manner as those which are pit fired. ▲

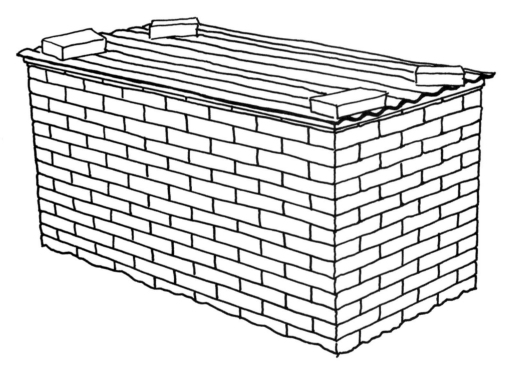

Rather than firing in a hole in the ground (with all its uncontrollable variables), the author built a brick-and-mortar chamber framed at the top with angle iron. Bisqued pots are placed close together on a bed of 3-4 inches of sawdust. A stick is used to scratch channels around the pots; then salt and copper sulfate are sprinkled into the channels. After wood is piled gently on top of the pots, a fire is started with newspaper and kindling. Once the flame is established, the chamber is covered with corrugated iron. Choking off the air supply is important in promoting color. Toward the end of the firing the corrugated iron is weighted down with bricks.

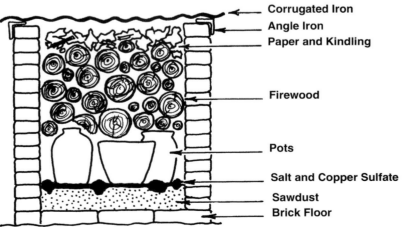

Corrugated Iron
Angle Iron
Paper and Kindling

Firewood

Pots

Salt and Copper Sulfate
Sawdust
Brick Floor

Pit Firing Branches Out

Smoke-Fired Pottery
by Jane Perryman

The technology that enables us to use high temperatures separates the potter from much of the joy and spontaneity of low-temperature smoking processes. During the last decade, a growing awareness and interest in "primitive techniques" have occurred partly as a reaction against the ever-increasing sophistication surrounding kiln technology and computerization, and partly against the preoccupation with high-fired stoneware and porcelain influenced by the Leach tradition. It should be emphasized that "primitive" does not imply coarse or unrefined; on the contrary, potters working with these firing techniques need to develop a high level of skill, sensitivity and patience to achieve successful results.

Smoke firing is based on the fact that when there is insufficient oxygen, the fuel, needing oxygen to burn, will combine with the oxides in the clay and leave a carbonaceous black surface. Several terms are used to describe the process. Some potters refer to it as "carbonizing" and others as "blackening"; i.e., producing blackware.

Like others with an aversion to the glazing process, the discovery of burnishing and smoke firing was a revelation to me ten years ago, and I have never looked back. The polished surfaces of pots richly

marked by smoke express qualities of softness, sensuality and earthiness that glazed work cannot convey. Tactile senses are stimulated and satiated by touching and holding these pots, and one experiences a feeling of timelessness through their associations with ancient pottery.

Some of the earliest examples of pottery using reduced and oxidized areas to express color contrasts are from the predynastic Egyptian potters (circa 3500

Jane Perryman smoothing the rim of a coil-built vessel to be smoke fired at her studio in Cambridge, England.

B.C.) in their black-topped, burnished redware. The contrast of red and black was achieved by carefully stacking pots so that one part of the pot was exposed to the reduction, while another part of it was shielded by a second pot placed over the top of it so it would remain oxidized.

Contemporary studio potters have drawn inspiration from primitive firing techniques that are still used in many parts of the world today, including India, Pakistan, Africa, South America, North America, and Papua, New Guinea. Firing is carried out without kilns, in the open or in pits, using locally available fuels, such as agricultural waste and animal dung. The resulting pots, which have developed over the centuries, display a high level of craftsmanship and aesthetics, harmonizing form, surface and function.

I went to Hornsey College of Art in London in the late 1960s, planning to specialize in textiles, but found myself in the Industrial Ceramics program, which concentrated on slip casting and mold making. To say it was the wrong course for me is a gross understatement; when I graduated, I felt as if all creativity had been knocked out of me. The most exciting aspect of art school was the "sit-in" of 1968, which I was very much involved in, but left-wing politics with its attendant

Perryman's vessels are constructed from flattened coils; the edges are scored and slipped to assure good joins.

For flared forms, a template is sometimes used to establish the curve.

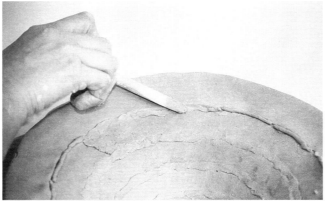

Small coils are added to strengthen each join, then pushed in firmly with a tool to ensure no air is trapped.

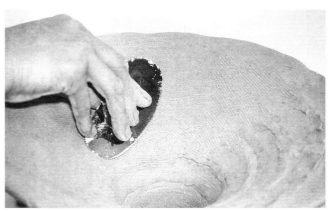

When leather hard, the form is refined and thinned by scraping with a metal rib.

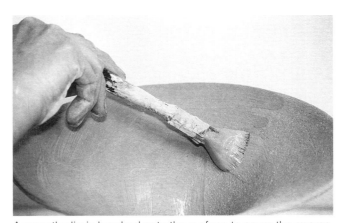

A smooth slip is brushed onto the surface to cover the coarse clay, then burnished with a spoon.

After a bisque firing, masking-tape patterns are applied, then covered with coarse slurry, which will resist the smoke.

ideologies meant choosing a career in teaching rather than "making art objects for elitist consumption." I taught full time in secondary schools for several years before feeling the need to make pots again. Joining a pottery cooperative was rather like beginning again; I decided to teach myself to throw and handbuild.

In 1979, a British Council Scholarship enabled me to spend a year at the Europees Keramisch Werkcentrum in Holland, an international center for potters to develop their work with unlimited resources. The time was spent exploring sculptural themes with slip-cast porcelain and experimenting with reduction glazes. This was followed by two years developing ideas in America.

Returning to Cambridge (where I still live), I was able to set up my own studio, and bought a ceramic fiber kiln. I have always been a "late starter," and at this stage, 12 years after leaving art school, I was still searching for my own way of working. When a friend showed me a burnished sawdust-fired pot, I felt an immediate affinity with it; here was a way to achieve a tactile surface of depth and great richness without glaze. I loved the soft quality created by low firing, and knew I

Pit Firing Branches Out

had at last found my way. This experience was reinforced by watching Siddig El'Nigoumi [see the January 1989 issue of CM] demonstrating his carbonizing techniques with newspaper at the South Wales Potters' Festival in 1983.

So began many years of adjusting clays and firing techniques through trial and error, with the attendant disappointments and jubilations. Gradually, I moved away from slip casting and into handbuilding. I began looking at low-fired pots from the archaeological and anthropological departments at museums. Forms became influenced by early British and French Celtic pots from the British Museum in London, which I returned to many times to draw and study. For several years, I incorporated a strongly defined shoulder into my bowls and vases—a direct reference to these Celtic pots.

Since I began smoke firing, my work has been vessel orientated, mostly bowls, vases and jugs. For many years, I used combinations of handbuilding methods—coiling, press molding and slab building—constructing the form in several sections and often completing it by adding a foot.

My first trip to India, at the beginning of 1990, was the catalyst to change. While studying yoga at the Iyengar Yoga Institute in Pune, I discovered a colony of potters living and working beside a busy roadway in the center of the city. I was particularly intrigued by a group of women potters who coil built tandoori ovens, by the beauty of the repetitive rhythms of coiling married with a complete economy of movement. It took 18 months to absorb this experience and translate it into my work by deciding to concentrate solely on coiling to create the form in one rather than several sections. This means the forms have become simpler and the defined shoulder has been replaced by a more organic curve.

My love of pattern is expressed by the decoration influenced by African textiles and carving, especially the raffia-pile textiles of the Congo (now Zaire). By penetrating into the surface, the smoke firing

In a stacked brick kiln, the pot is surrounded by wood shavings.

During the firing (about three hours), the shavings burn away, leaving a residue of ash.

The tape either burns away or lifts up, opening the masked areas to smoke; the resist slurry is removed by scraping, revealing lighter, unsmoked areas.

Flared vase, 13½ inches in diameter, coil-built T Material and porcelain, slipped and burnished, bisqued, masked and smoke fired.

creates patterns of great intensity, which become part of the form. I keep a sketchbook for trying out new shapes and patterns, but as the process of handbuilding is slow, new forms tend to evolve slowly and often unconsciously.

Pots are made from a mixture of 2 parts T Material (coarse stoneware) and 1 part porcelain. I begin with a flat base and often use a cardboard template as a rough guide. "Coils" are in fact rolled by hand and then flattened to about ¼ inch; they are built up carefully, with score marks and slurry in between to secure a good bond. Thin coils of clay are pushed in between the larger coils to ensure they are joined together well. This takes a long time, but I rarely get cracks around the coiling lines. When leather hard, the shape is refined through scraping and beating, and lastly sponged. A ball clay slip (5 parts Hymod SMD Ball Clay with 1 part clay body) is colored with oxides or commercial stains and brushed on in several layers. When the pot is sufficiently dry, I burnish with a spoon and pebble, then polish with a plastic-covered pad.

Bisque firing is to around 980°C (1800°F). The surface is then patterned with masking tape and covered with a crank clay slurry, which will act as a resist

against the smoke. The tape will either burn away or lift up from the surface, allowing these areas to absorb smoke.

A simple brick construction forms the kiln; it can be adjusted to accommodate the size and number of pots easily. Fuel is mostly coarse wood shavings because they burn faster than sawdust, and that is important as I live in the center of Cambridge. Over the years, I have learned that I can achieve adequate carbonization with less fuel.

Smoke-fired vase, coil built, slipped and burnished, approximately 13 inches in height, by Jane Perryman.

Pots are laid on several inches of shavings, then surrounded by and covered with additional densely packed shavings. The kiln is set alight, covered with a sheet of metal and left for 2–4 hours. Sometimes I fire in a metal trash can with newspaper, which can be finished as quickly as 10–15 minutes. Some pots need several firings to achieve satisfactory results; some pots are never satisfactory and can be re-oxidized and smoked again.

After the firing, the slurry is cleaned away. Sometimes it falls off easily; other times it is removed with a scalpel. A coat of beeswax will seal the surface.

The excitement and anticipation surrounding the risks and unpredictability are important aspects of smoke firing. Results can give great joy or great disappointment, and it is this element of not quite being in control, of letting go of preconceptions, that is so appealing. After many hours of slow, controlled making, it is a liberating feeling to "give" the pot to the fire, to be directly involved with the firing, to see the flames, and to see and smell the smoke. Although the technique is simple, success depends on many years of experimentation and observation, of trial-and-error and the acceptance of failure as a tool for learning. ▲

Jeff Kell

by Maryalice Yakutchik

Jeff Kell, Reading, Pennsylvania.

They are made on a potter's wheel in the dusty basement studio of his Reading, Pennsylvania, row house, but Jeff Kell's vessels achieve their identity through pit firing in a country field. There, bisqueware is placed in a 55-gallon drum punched full of holes, "which sits in a 4-foot-deep pit dug into the bank of a hill," Kell explains. "This natural shelter protects the drum from the wind, captures heat and allows for more even temperature while firing.

"Initially, I tried burning myriad materials—wood chunks, sawdust, grass, leaves, etc.—in an attempt to attain even temperature," he says. "But they all resulted in inconsistent fires and cracked vessels.

"Finally, I tried straw and have found it to be the ideal fuel for my purpose. It can be spread evenly and so yields consistent heat over the entire vessel, which helps prevent cracking. I continuously add straw so the fire quickly attains,

then stays at a temperature intense enough to permit color development.

"Exciting, unexpected things happen, but always within certain parameters, which I control."

Kell's current work is influenced by early impressions of and continuing ex-

posure to primitive cultures. "Sometimes I am made aware that what I see or read directly influences my work," he adds.

Thrown in sections at the wheel, his vessels range in height from 15 to 60 inches, and in diameter from 12 to 22 inches. Using a heavily grogged, commercial sculpture clay "helps prevent slumping when I throw large forms. Additionally, this body [made of approximately 35% kaolin, 35% fireclay, and 30% grog] resists cracking (in the uneven temperatures that occur during straw firing) better than other clay bodies with which I have experimented."

Once the sections are assembled, altered and textured, he completes the form with slip trailing. "Although application of the slip is the most spontaneous part of the process, I still control the movement, still plan for it, to a degree," he says. "I want fluid lines that take the eye first horizontally across the vessel, then draw it down dramatically.

"Ritual Vessel II," 26 inches in height, thrown and slab built, fired in straw.

"Classic Vessel," 2 feet high, with impressing, trailed slips and sprayed copper matt.

"Prelibation of Deity," 41 inches in height, heavily grogged sculpture clay, thrown and slab built, impressed, trailed with slip, bisqued to Cone 06, sprayed with copper matt solution, straw fired.

Basic shapes are thrown at the wheel in Kell's basement studio.

Thrown sections are assembled, topped with a thrown and slab-built lid, then textured by impressing and trailing.

Bisqueware is misted with a copper matt solution, then fired with straw inside a metal drum punched full of holes.

What allows me a balance between planned and spontaneous action is the consistency of the slip, which must be fairly stiff, so that it holds three-dimensional shape."

Trailing slip is made from equal parts of the same clay body used to make the vessels and an earthenware clay. This is subsequently passed through an 80-mesh screen.

Once the vessels are bone dry, they are bisque fired to Cone 06. To enhance color development during firing, a copper matt solution is sprayed—with an ordinary plant mister—onto each vessel. (The recipe originally came from *"The Copper Matt Finish"* published in the April 1985 Ceramics Monthly. It is 10% Ferro frit 3110 and 90% copper carbonate. To this, Kell usually adds 1%–2% red iron oxide.)

"I've experimented with an airbrush," he explains, "but that rendered regular results that looked too contrived. With a mister, I get intermittent little drops and the occasional big splash. The copper, in the atmosphere of the straw firing, gives the vessels a wide range of color, predominantly blue and rust tints, but also some unexpected ones: muted shades of pale peach through steel blue/gray with some dark rust and orange spots. The copper starts to react at very low temperatures (around 700°F), which is important since the straw fire probably doesn't get much above 1000°F.

"Fire is an elemental force, straightforward, powerful and primitive," Kell says. "I enjoy standing over and feeding it, and watching as it changes the vessel within." ▲

Smoke and Color

by Glenn Spangler

The only thing interesting about that day was that it looked like it might rain. It was the end of August, and the rains don't usually come until October.

Because I found myself wandering around the studio, trying to decide which tasks were the least undesirable, I knew it was time to take a break from production. When this happens, and there are no pressing deadlines, I give myself permission to use work time for research.

The experiment was directed toward producing a contrasting black-and-white pattern on bare porcelain bisqueware. In past weeks, I had placed pots in a pit fire to smoke carbon deep into the clay. Hot spots were allowed to develop toward the end of the firing to burn off carbon in some places and reveal the stark white porcelain body.

The first tests had been inconclusive and uninspiring. The fire always burned too hot, producing mostly white or light gray surfaces. I had tried sawdust firing to get and keep more carbon in the clay, but that had not yet yielded dense blacks or clean whites.

On that August day, I decided to try burning pine shavings. After a ring of holes was punched around the bottom of a 3-gallon can, a bowl was nestled inside it on 4 inches of pine shavings. Next, the bowl was covered completely with another 5 or 6 inches of shavings, which were then ignited. When there were glowing ashes, the can was covered with a round Formica sink cutout. This lid was propped slightly open with a small twig about half the diameter of a pencil to create a draft from the ring of holes punched around the bottom of the can. It was starting to sprinkle as I lit the shavings. "A little rain won't hurt," I thought. "The can will be covered."

After making sure the smoke billowed from the opening between the lid and the top of the can, I waited with a potter's enforced patience. As I ate lunch, checking the firing through the open door of the studio, the rain increased to a downpour. A closer inspection showed water running into the holes around the bottom of the can.

"Well, that's it for this test," I thought. "Wet shavings don't burn. I'll dump this and start over."

Then I stopped. The fire was still burning. "So what if it's getting wet? Let's see what happens if it goes all the way."

Not being able to resist a little cautious meddling, I moved the can to dry ground without disturbing the fire. Two hours later, I returned to look.

Sitting in the black-and-white ash was a very smoky bowl. When I picked it up and looked at the side that had been in the ashes, I felt the excitement of discovery that keeps me in this business.

The rain had soaked the shavings just up to the bowl, which had absorbed water wherever it had come into contact with the wet shavings. With the water came all the soluble materials from the wood, which were deposited in globs and streaks. The smoky atmosphere had reacted with the soluble materials from the wood, forming a mottled pattern; while the damp porcelain resisted the smoke, leaving a white halo around the pattern.

It had turned into a very interesting day. I covered the bottom of another can with presoaked shavings, placed a bowl on top of them, and found the process was repeatable without the need for rain.

Because soluble materials were the important factor, I surmised any alteration of the amount present would change the results. In the next weeks, several ways of varying the solubles were tested.

Some interesting results were achieved in concentrating the solubles by soaking the shavings in hot water for an hour before setting up the firing. This produced darker and more colorful background patterns. Other soluble materials, such as 10% copper sulfate and 10% silver nitrate, were added by pouring them over the shavings. Both of those also darkened the pattern, and the copper produced a green tint in the surrounding halo.

I soon realized that any water soluble color could be added, including watercolors or fabric paint. Fabric paint seems to work best. After careful cleaning and air drying, the patterns produced by fabric paint can be made permanent by heating the pot to 250°F. The surface can then be protected by waterproofing the pot with bisque seal or heavy-duty Chem Stop. [For a list of distributors, write Chem Stop Manufacturing and Sales Corporation, 9920 East Flora Vista Avenue, Bellflower, California 90706.

Color can also be added by using insoluble materials such as iron oxide. A light wash of pure red iron oxide (2 teaspoons per quart), sprayed on the shavings just before placing the pot into the can, produces a pink background.

As I thought about the whole process—the things that worked, didn't work or sort of worked—I remembered something my father said about farming. "There's nothing like a good early rain to get things growing, but it means you'll have to pull a lot of weeds that spring." ▲

"Black Water Coral," 3½ inches in height, porcelain, with iron wash, smoked on wet pine shavings.

"Greenwood Tea," 2¾ inches high, fired on pine shavings soaked in fabric paint.

"Fire Burst," 4 inches high, sawdust fired on wet shavings soaked in fabric paint.

"Smoking Rain," sawdust-fired porcelain, 3 inches in height, by Glenn Spangler.

Madhvi Subrahmanian

Untitled, 13 inches in diameter, coil-built earthenware with terra sigillata, fired to Cone 08, then smoked in newspaper, by Madhvi Subrahmanian, Mumbai, India.

Smoked, coil-built earthenware vessel, 18 inches in height.

Indian ceramist Madhvi Subrahmanian coil builds her vessel forms from earthenware. Brushed with terra sigillata and glazes, they are typically fired several times (as many as five) to Cone 04.

Some pieces are fired only to Cone 08, then smoked with newspaper in a tin drum. On these, she enjoys "working and reworking the surface, layering it with terra sigillatas, glazes, and smoke firing it several times until it enhances the form, just as life itself is enriched with every layer of experience."

Derived from the functional pot, her work has moved toward the sculptural vessel. "The sensuous plasticity of clay is what drew me into the world of ceramics," she explains.

"Having started as a functional potter, I have a deep appreciation of the rhythm of the wheel and of everyday objects. These ordinary intimate objects have helped me understand their potential to express meaning far beyond their mundane functions. My current work is the result of questioning and searching for the various meanings of a container."

After studying for four years with Ray Meeker and Deborah Smith at the Golden Bridge Pottery in Pondicherry, India, she came to the United States in 1989 to earn a M.F.A. degree at the Southern Methodist University in Texas.

Having lived in several parts of the world, Subrahmanian recognizes that her "work in many ways is the result of change—the challenge of new opportunities and limitations that comes with every move and new phase of life." ▲

Gabriele Koch

German-born Gabriele Koch, who now lives and works in England, creates burnished and smoked hand-built vessels.

"My initial desire to work in clay was kindled in Spain," Koch recalls. "Repeated visits left deep impressions: an open desertlike landscape with simple horizon lines and strong earth colors from black to ocher to red; and the physical confrontation with heat, earth and water—the potter's raw materials."

Her current work is built from flat coils of a T-material/porcelain mixture, sponged to raise the "tooth," brushed with colored slip and burnished. She is "concerned with the exploration and interpretation of architectural form, which in turn leads to reconsidering surface qualities and the relationship between form and color."

Writing about Koch's work, Tony Birks observes that a pot "is a membrane between an inside space and an enclosing space. Gabriele's work can be seen in terms of the tension between the two; in her most recent tower forms, she has been linking the inner and outer spaces more closely with small orifices, slits and cuts, thus revealing the substance of the pot, and leading the eye inside.

"Because of the labor-intensive nature of her technique," Birks notes, "she can produce only a limited number of pots per year. The studio, where she works without assistants, will normally contain five or six pots at various stages, and it is here that the form and the surface texture are completed."

Following an initial firing to 950°C (1742°F), the pots are smoked in a saw-dust firing, "in which oxygen starvation and the mixture of different types of timber dust both play a part," explains Birks. "Cloud formations growing up through air currents" create the one-of-a-kind patterns. ▲

"Red Form with Dimple," approximately 14 inches in height, porcelain with T-material, smoke fired.

"Red Bell," approximately 16 inches in height, coil-built T-material, burnished and smoke fired.

"Tall Blue Tower," approximately 16 inches in height, smoked porcelain and T-material, by Gabriele Koch, London.

REDISCOVERING THE KILN:
Saggar firing

A potter from the 19th century watching a 21st-century potter preparing a saggar would be completely baffled. He would have used saggars to protect pottery from the gasses released by dirty fuels such as coal—thus, the modern technique of surrounding pots in a saggar with combustible and volatile materials would seem entirely backwards.

Using a saggar inside a kiln is essentially a variation on firing in a barrel or brick chamber. Instead of lighting the fuel in the barrel directly, the barrel, or saggar, is loaded into the kiln and the kiln is fired to a high enough temperature to burn the material in the saggar. Traditionally, a saggar is made of clay and resembles a lidded canister. However, most modern potters who saggar fire find it more convenient and versatile to build a saggar inside the kiln using bricks. The bricks can be stored more compactly than a collection of saggars, and can be used to build chambers of various sizes within the kiln.

The advantages of firing in a saggar are that the temperature of the firing can be controlled more precisely, by monitoring it with cones, and a higher temperature can be achieved than what is possible when firing in a barrel or pit. The higher temperature may allow for more vivid colors or deeper blacks, particularly when there is only a small amount of ware to be fired. Another benefit to firing in a saggar is that the potter doesn't have to rely on air flowing through the packed saggar to keep the combustibles burning—the heat of the kiln takes care of that. Therefore, the placement of pots in relation to the volatile and combustible materials can be more precise. Depending on the desired results, the saggar can be closed up quite tightly, or chinks can be left between the bricks to allow the material to burn away more completely.

The artists profiled in this chapter make evident the variety and versatility of saggar firing. A poten-tial drawback to saggar firing is addressed by Macy Dorf with suggestions for reducing the problem of smoke emission. Obviously, the main limiting factor to the technique is the fact that the technological bar is raised a bit higher—it is not possible to saggar fire without a kiln. While it may be possible, it is not advisable to saggar fire in an electric kiln, because the smoke will damage the elements. Therefore, saggar firing is an option only for potters with access to a gas kiln. The results are exciting enough, however, that any potter with an interest in pit firing will eventually want to beg, borrow, or buy a suitable kiln to try this tempting technique.

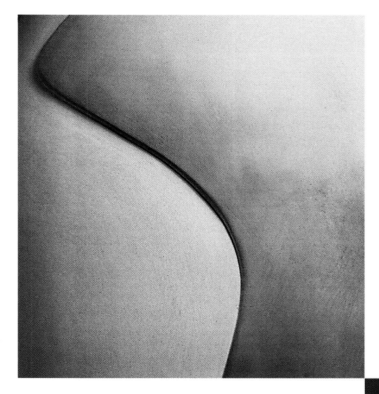

Saggar-fired vessel, 14 inches high, wheel thrown, with iron sulfate wash, by R. Bede Clarke.

"A Burning Passion," 24 inches in height, with 5% copper carbonate slip, sprayed with salt water solution, saggar fired.

Low-Temperature Salt/Saggar Firing

by R. Bede Clarke

Traditionally, saggars have been used to protect pottery from the effects of direct flame, and in the case of wood and coal firing, from ash and debris. For the purpose of low-temperature salt-firing, saggars do just the opposite. That is, they act as an enclosure (within a fuel-burning kiln) in which the effects of the fire are encouraged and courted by packing a variety of organic matter and rubbish around the pots.

My work with saggars began with an interest in the low-fire salt process developed by Paul Soldner. Salts were introduced by soaking bisque-fired pots in saline solutions and by sprinkling salts throughout the kiln. Predominant colors were pinks, oranges and violets. After a year of research in this area, I felt the need for a more

substantial palette and so began experimenting with packing combustible materials around the pots to produce dark carbonaceous areas.

Throw only a couple of saggars and you'll realize this was not a solution. The problem being: clay saggars are short-lived and so the time and expense of making them are recurring. Besides, I wanted to make large pots which require even bigger saggars. A simple solution was to build the saggars from hard firebrick.

The advantages of using brick are: they last for years; saggars may be built to any size; and any gaps may be adjusted to control the flame pattern and atmosphere. Also, brick saggars may be capped with kiln shelves or left partially or completely open. Obviously, the degree to

which the saggar is sealed affects colors achieved through oxidation/reduction.

Because no glaze is applied before firing, surface effects vary widely, depending upon clay color and texture. White bodies seem to encourage a greater range of color when combined with applications of slips, oxides, soluble salts, commercial stains and underglazes. Dark clays lend themselves to deep muted tones, while porcelain is most reactive, rendering delicate blushes as well as intense flashes of color. It is best to simply make some pots out of a variety of bodies and see which you prefer.

With thrown forms, clay strength is not an issue. However, large handbuilt pieces are susceptible to cracking due to the uneven temperatures created by burning materials within the saggar.

Wanting a multipurpose clay body, I settled on the following recipe:

White Salt/Saggar Clay Body
(Cone 010–04)

Talc	15.0%
Wollastonite	5.0
A.P. Green Fireclay	40.0
Tennessee Ball Clay	25.0
Fine Grog	7.5
Medium Grog	7.5
	100.0%

To a 100-pound batch, add 1 quart vinegar to facilitate aging. An additional 5%–10% coarse grog is beneficial for crack prevention in large forms.

As with many aspects of saggar firing, the question of bisque firing is highly conditional. One advantage of bisquing is that large handbuilt forms and pots with fragile additions are less susceptible to cracking and breakage. Another is that oxides may be brushed and rubbed more aggressively onto bisqued pieces; and, of course, only bisqueware may be soaked in brine. In favor of single firing: raw clay and slips are generally more responsive to the effects of the fire. Additionally, there are the obvious savings in firing time and expense.

My initial experiments with slips were hampered by the huge amount of salts I was using on and around the pots. The slips literally were eaten away. Since exercising restraint with the salts, I have found tremendous potential for slip in saggar firing. With one clay body and a variety of slips, a range of surfaces may be explored.

Base White Slip
(Cone 010–06)

Gerstley Borate	25.0%
Kaolin	40.0
Flint	35.0
	100.0%

Apply thinly onto green- or bisqueware. For volatile reds, greens and purples, add 5% copper carbonate. This copper variation is most reactive when not bisqued prior to the saggar firing.

Textured White Slip
(Cone 06)

Gerstley Borate	17.7%
Zircopax	4.4
Ball Clay	35.4
Bentonite	7.1
Kaolin	17.7
Flint	17.7
	100.0%

Apply to leather-hard ware.

Oxides and commercial stains may be sprayed and brushed onto greenware or bisqued ware. Additionally, oxides may be sprinkled around the floor of the saggar next to the pots. Particularly valuable here are any of the forms of copper. Underglazes may be thinned, and as such become like stains. The resulting colors can be quite subtle as the underglazes are partially obscured by flashing within the saggar.

In the earthenware range, salt does not form a glaze as in high firing. Rather, the vaporized sodium reacts with alumina and silica in the clay to produce blushes of color. Common table and rock salt are good sources of sodium. Soda ash may also be used, but it fluxes at low temperatures and forms a glaze, something I've tried to avoid. A strong solution of 4 cups of salt to 1 gallon of water may be mixed then sprayed or brushed onto the pots. When used over thin washes of oxides, many colors will result. Soluble salts such as the sulfates of barium, iron and copper may be applied in a weaker solution of ½–2 cups per gallon of water. Iron sulfate has been a personal favorite for its color range of light orange to rust red, depending on the solution's iron concentration.

Use caution when handling soluble salts as they are potentially toxic. Wear a respirator and rubber gloves, because solubles can pass directly through the skin. The safest methods of application are brushing and pouring.

Of all the variables in salt/saggar firing, the most critical are stacking the saggar and the firing temperature. I have found the best range to be Cone 012–04. Before Cone 012 the salts do not react, and beyond Cone 04 colors tend to brown out. Also, with higher firing the clay becomes more vitreous and thus more susceptible to cracking.

When building a brick saggar around ware, care is taken not to impede heat flow by blocking the burners or flue.

Carbonaceous and masking materials are added as the saggar is raised; an oval saggar is more stable than a rectangle.

Salts and oxides are sprinkled on and around the pots at various levels during saggar construction.

Packing materials include charcoal, broken firebrick, salt-soaked vermiculite, and wood shavings.

In a typical saggar setting, the pots are surrounded with packing materials up to their rims.

Once the saggar is capped with kiln shelves, bisque- or greenware may be loaded on top.

If large amounts of charcoal are used in the saggar, it is best to fire below Cone 010 due to the additional heat given off by the briquettes. For a Cone 010 saggar firing of bisqued pots, a typical firing time in a 25-cubic-foot kiln is from five to six hours. For raw pots the kiln is preheated overnight, with Cone 010 reached in eight to nine hours. Bisque- and greenware may be fired in the same load, following the slower firing schedule for raw pots. I normally measure temperature with cones placed on top of the saggar lid.

The choice of materials used in the saggar, to a great extent, determines the final result. The following is a list of materials with the results characteristically achieved in the firing:

Charcoal briquettes will contribute strong darks and add temperature to the saggar. Wood charcoal works best. Crushed briquettes produce more subtle markings.

Vermiculite, when soaked in salt water, leaves haloed impressions on the clay surface.

Broken softbrick acts as a masking material and creates openness which encourages flashing as the flame moves through the saggar.

Seaweed contributes salt, and leaves raised textural markings.

Sawdust and wood shavings are valuable marking agents when soaked in salt water.

Salts are the principal influencer of color when added in a proportion of 2–5 pounds NaCl (rock and/or table) or Epsom salt per 12-cubic-foot saggar.

A good source for additional materials is an animal feed store, where you can find hay, rice hulls and oat chaff. All of these probably will give best results when soaked in brine. Soaked materials should be thoroughly dried prior to setting the saggar.

When firing a gas kiln, the saggar may be built out to the bag walls. It may fill the kiln so long as the burners are not impeded and the heat flow is not interrupted by obstructing the flue. I have used an electric kiln only once with this process and am somewhat biased against them for saggar work. However, if that is what is available, then the saggar may be built to within an inch or so of the kiln walls. Salt vapors will decrease the life of the elements, but at low temperatures salt vapors have a negligible effect on firebrick. In fact, low-temperature salt/saggar firings may be alternated with more traditional glaze and bisque firings. Due to harmful gases given off during this process, fire only in a well-ventilated area. When working around a kiln giving off salt (hydrochloric acid) vapors, use a charcoal acid gas cartridge in your respirator.

Begin building the saggar by placing two or three courses of firebrick on their 9-inch edges. Hard firebrick are best to use and should be lapped

to create an interlocking wall. Brick may be leveled with a mixture of equal parts kaolin, silica and sand. Pots are then placed on the floor shelves or elevated on firebrick in order to use all the saggar space. Allow for a bit of space around the pots so that they are touched by materials on all sides. Then begin packing materials around the pots, building the saggar up as you go. To achieve a good setting of materials, I try to be sensitive to the following three considerations:

Consistency—all the various materials should be evenly spaced and layered, so as to create a unified packing and to avoid "blank spots" on the pots.

Dark and light—a balance of dark and light areas can be achieved by even distribution of noncarbonaceous and masking materials (vermiculite and broken firebrick) and carbonaceous materials (sawdust, charcoal, etc.). Broken firebrick will generally make up a third to one-half of the setting. The remainder is composed of a blend of materials in proportions determined by results desired.

Interior surfaces—concern for all visible surfaces means packing the interior or the neck of a pot with the same care you use to pack the outside.

At its worst, saggar firing can become just a surface to cover up pots. At its best, it can strike a balance between the mark of the individual potter and the expression of natural forces. ▲

Decorating with Volatile Materials in Saggars

by Ruth Allan

Historically, saggars (heavy, stackable, coarse fireclay containers) have been used to protect pottery from flying ash, reduction and unwanted fumes in fuel-burning kilns; they also have served as a means of vertical stacking without shelves and posts. Contemporary saggar firing transposes the concept of protection, exposing the work to combustibles and volatile materials, while protecting the kiln.

In 1984, my work was all Cone 10 reduction or raku. Living in relative isolation on the desert side of Washington State (where the Columbia River touches the edge of the Cascade Mountains), I had limited contacts with other professional potters, but found the strong flashes of color and ethereal blushes of saggar work fascinating. So that fall I invited Richard Mahaffey over from Tacoma to do a weekend workshop at Wenatchee Valley College. He achieved irresistible results with a loaded saggar inside a portable raku kiln.

Disastrous best describes my first dozen saggar firing attempts. It was not unusual to have all but one of the pots crack in a load. Having encountered other potters who were unwilling to give specific information, I was hesitant to ask Mahaffey for more—even now that I knew the right questions—so I muddled along. I later learned that he believes in freely sharing information.

When I was ready for my first saggar firing, the snow was 2 feet deep, it was -5° F and bad weather was on the way. Using an indoor, 20-cubic-foot, updraft kiln, instead of the raku kiln, seemed very attractive. Earlier I had decided building a brick saggar, rather than throwing lidded saggars, was the way to create maximum firing space with minimal exertion.

The saggar was (and still is) built of K-26 firebrick standing

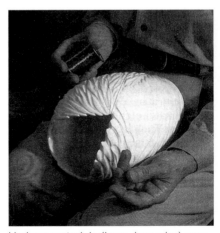
For etched patterns, the wheel-thrown porcelain pots are burnished, dried completely and brushed with wax.

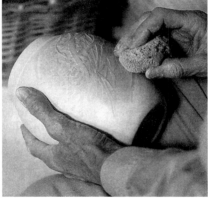
A wet sponge is then rubbed over the dry wax designs to remove a thin layer of the exposed porcelain.

Etched bowl, 13 inches wide, with masking-tape accents and carbon from wood shavings packed around the rim.

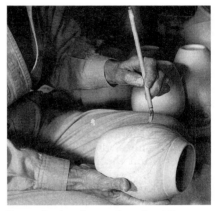
Various materials (here, iron wire) may be placed on the bisqued pot to achieve particular effects in the saggar firing.

Tinned copper wire may yield black, black with a green halo, white or pink; and masking tape attracts minerals.

Saggar-fired porcelain jar, 15 inches in height, burnished, with tinned copper wire and masking-tape lines.

on end, with mullite shelves on edge to protect the back of the kiln, silicon carbide shelves on top, then another chamber of bricks and shelves. Packed inside with the pots were copper or zinc wires for local color, sawdust and table salt (on the saggar floor). The kiln was warmed overnight, then air and gas were increased gradually at the burners to reach Cone 1 (kiln floor reading, outside the saggar). Some color and lots of cracking occurred.

Then I tried leaving a space between bricks. No luck. Next I tried stacking bricks as tightly as possible, using a grogged stoneware gasket between brick tops and lid. All in all, what I had was a great setup for destroying pots.

I was using bisqued, Cone 10 porcelain and stoneware; both cracked. The causes were varied: thermal shock from sawdust igniting too soon, from any contact with salt, contact with other pots, and contact with shelves and saggar walls. In spite of these losses, the peach to russet, plum to gray, cream to black coloring lured me on.

I conceived many strategies to overcome cracking and improve color. Fractures from the feet were eliminated by setting pots in shallow dishes filled with sand, or on a softbrick. Salt-induced cracks were prevented by confining salt to high-fire cups set in small, low dishes of sand in the hot, upper areas of the saggar so that it could "bomb" the pots below. A ceramic fiber blanket on pots seemed to trap more of the mineral fumes from the wires, thus increasing color intensity, but it could also insulate against color. Also, if the fiber touched the liquid salt, it could act like a wick, causing the pot's destruction.

Lowering the firing temperature to Cone 04 improved the color and reduced stresses. This allowed me to pack more efficiently by setting pots on one another. I tried sawdust, wood shavings, wood chips and even dried cow dung for organic material. Wood shavings, whatever the variety of tree, worked best. The tighter the pack, the more carbon was trapped in the pots. If too tight, however, the shavings insulated against color.

Though improvements were many, there was still significant loss from thermal shock. My ideas for solutions seemed exhausted, so I called Mahaffey. He provided such key suggestions as elimination of overnight warm-up, starting with substantial flame and making the saggar as airtight as possible, even using kiln putty (almost-stiff kiln wash) to seal small gaps between bricks. That eliminated the fractures from thermal shock.

By then the tops of the K-26 bricks used for the saggar were distorted from contact with the stoneware gasket. Some hardbrick that had been salvaged years before from the local Alcoa plant worked better. (Scrounging there is no longer allowed because an employee hurt himself while doing it and sued the company.) These were made with a groove along the bottom spine and a corresponding hump on the top that ensures a more airtight seal, as does the square saggar format.

Because regular Cone 10 reduction firings are done in this same kiln, the saggar must be frequently constructed and removed. About 5 cubic feet in capacity, it accommodates work up to 22 inches tall and 17 inches wide. I start by cleaning out the kiln, removing the kiln radiants and bag walls (optional). Every time the saggar is built, a fresh ⅛-inch-thick layer of alumina hydrate powder is spread on the floor and old shelves placed on it; any cracks between shelves are filled with alumina hydrate or kiln putty. Shelf size determines the size of the saggar, but it may be built all the way to the bag walls. A mullite shelf propped against the back wall protects the kiln and forms the back of the saggar.

Ceramic fiber gaskets (½ inch thick and 3 inches wide) are used at the edges of the bottom shelves as a seal on which to place the bricks, at the back of the saggar where bricks butt against the mullite shelves, and where the front and side saggar bricks meet. When building the saggar walls, maintain a tight structure, filling cracks with kiln putty. The saggar height depends on the size of work being fired. Along the top brick course, a ceramic fiber gasket (1 inch thick and 3 inches wide) is placed to seal the lid (two high-alumina shelves). There is not as much mineral buildup on high-alumina shelves as on those made of silicon carbide.

Preparation of the pots evolved, just as the saggar building and firing did. Various materials and objects are used to produce a variety of surface effects. My current work involves three stages:

Stage one: The surfaces of wheel-thrown porcelain vessels are burnished. Some are then carved and burnished again with a small piece of 4-mil polyethylene plastic; others are burnished and water etched. Etching is done when a burnished pot is bone dry. Wax resist is painted in patterns that suggest supple vegetation, and the unwaxed surface is wiped away with a wet sponge (a Carlton Ball technique). A number of depths can be achieved with successive drying, waxing and sponging—no-tech sandblasting! The etched area is burnished with a dry cellulose sponge.

Be aware that touching burnished areas before they are completely dry can capture fingerprints that will be highlighted by saggar firing. This could be used to advantage, but it sure ruins a pot for those to whom fingerprints are not a turn-on.

Stage two: After a Cone 02 bisque firing, various materials are placed on or attached to the surface of the pots. Each material has a range of potential effects, of which none or all can occur in a firing. Some may work well most of the time, but not always.

Iron wire (0.0009 inch in diameter, with a composition of 99% iron and 0.05% sulfur) at low temperatures can cause strong brown lines with blushes of apricot, peach and pink—sometimes. At higher temperatures, the blush becomes mauve—sometimes. Too hot, and the lines become flat brown with tan blush—always.

Tinned copper wire (Richard Mahaffey's favorite) can yield strong black lines, black with a green halo, white, pink or no lines at all. If these strong black lines are too distracting they can be eliminated by refiring.

Steel wool can be positioned near work to increase general color. When it is touching the surface, dark brown flashing occurs. A strand around a pot can give an elegant twisting line/blush or less-than-lovely "scritches and smurges."

Mild steel filings (from a machine shop) make strong staccato marks, or contribute to the general mineral-rich atmosphere in the saggar.

Masking tape (Is that a guffaw? Now, this really works, except when it doesn't.) Pressed onto the burnished surfaces attracts minerals. I use it in a pattern that suggests vegetation similar to the water-etched vessels. Different brands cause different colors: Tuck tape yields the full range of cream, yellow, peach, pink, mauve, lavender, russet and brown; Nashua tape, gray and black. This trait was discovered after using tape to secure wires at the bottom of pots.

Wood shavings can be manipulated as another option. Modest amounts placed around the work in the saggar result in gray-blue-lavender-black. Or you can fill a large pot with shavings, layer smaller pots inside with ample shavings between them, pile more shavings around the rim and hold them down with an inverted bowl. Not only do the small pots emerge a

Wheel-thrown porcelain jar. 8 inches in height, with "blushes" from steel wool placed on the burnished surface.

Carved and burnished porcelain jar, 18 inches in height, saggar fired, by Ruth Allan, Wenatchee, Washington.

In a saggar firing, strands of steel wool (positioned on the pot or trailed down a nearby post) increase color from volatile materials; wherever the steel wool touches the burnished porcelain surface, dark brown flashing occurs.

Carved, leather-hard pots are sponged, then burnished with a piece of 4-mil plastic; touching burnished surfaces before they are dry can capture fingerprints that will be highlighted by saggar firing.

magnificent black, but the interior and top of the large pot where the bowl held in the carbon (a saggar within a saggar) can yield the same lustrous ebony.

I have tried many processes over the years, but the preceding are the most useful to me at the moment. If I have an idea, I give it more than one try. Persistence, willingness to experiment with unlikely things, can pay off. Acrylic lace transferred its pattern onto a student's mask once.

Stage three: Loading the saggar is the most important part of the whole process. Great care and much thought go into positioning each pot, volatile material (Mason stains tend to fade away), post, support and spacer. If the pack is too tight, the lower center of the saggar is a dead zone, with little carbon and no color. Materials that color one pot may trash another. Plates, tiles, little pads of ceramic fiber can be placed between pots to cushion them in a vertical stack. Every change modifies and affects color potential.

I still raise the work off the saggar floor by using dishes of sand or a softbrick to allow pouring ½-inch mounds of salt on the floor around each. Sometimes iron filings are placed on top of the salt. A piece of steel wool can be trailed down a tall post so it is near the work; I may also lean a juicy iron filing against the same post and hope they both will fume color to the pots.

Posts are also used to elevate salt cups into the higher temperature areas when no shelves are used. The pots are never allowed to

touch posts or cups—liquefied salt is deadly to them if the cup leaks. About 3 pounds of table or sea salt are used per firing.

A redundancy of coloring agents ensures results from at least one. Wood shavings are added as the stacking progresses, easing off in the upper third. The load is topped off with old saggar-fired plates and tiles that have accumulated minerals. These seem to shield heat and contribute to color distribution. The whole top of the pack is tucked in with a ceramic fiber blanket to help insulate against excessive heat from the lid. The two shelves that form the lid are placed on the ceramic fiber gasket that tops the saggar walls. The center crack between shelves is insulated with ceramic fiber weighted in place with posts.

It often takes five hours to load the saggar. After watching me do a saggar stack, one of my students said, "No wonder it takes so long to load; you actually think when you do it."

Temperature is critical to good color response. Cone 012 to Cone 04 seems to yield a good palette. Below that, usually gray, lavender, blue and black develop without warm colors. Above that, only brown, tan and cream remain. After more than 140 saggar firings, I no longer use cones, just timed gas and air increases.

For a typical firing, gas is started at 3 inches and air at 60% with bottom plugs in and the top door plug out. I use this setting for two hours, then turn the gas to 4 inches and the blowers to 80%, remove bottom plugs, install top plug in the door, and set heavy reduction. After firing at this setting

Rediscovering The Kiln

The saggar is built from mullite shelves and interlocking bricks; strips of ceramic fiber are used to seal gaps.

Most pots are elevated on dishes of sand so that salt, iron filings and steel wool can be positioned under/around them.

Wood shavings held on top of a pot by an inverted dish (right front) will produce a carbon-black rim.

Tiles between works help stabilize the stack; note the dishes of salt and iron filings positioned throughout the saggar.

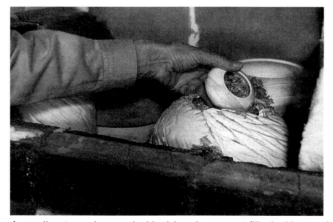

A small pot can be nestled inside a larger pot filled with wood shavings for a saggar within a saggar.

Mineral-rich tiles and dishes top the load; a ceramic fiber blanket overall will help insulate against excessive heat.

for three and a half hours, I turn off the kiln. A shorter saggar takes a little less time; a taller one takes a little more.

Each kiln fires differently and every change can modify the procedure. Ours has been in use since 1966, so we treated it to new burner fans last spring. This cut saggar firing time by 30 minutes, but there was no time change for Cone 10 reduction.

Uncovering the contents the next day is not just exciting, but a learning and often humbling experience. It's analysis time. If the result is unexpected, what caused it? If interesting, how can it be reproduced? Surprises are not automatically dismissed because they do not fit expectations. These can offer new directions.

Care is taken to avoid smudges from wood shavings (now charcoal) as the work is lifted out. Such marks may be difficult to remove without refiring—a pink eraser helps. The best pots are dusted and vacuumed, then dipped in Thompson's Water Seal and polished with a soft cloth. Ceramic Seal spray is better for rough surfaces, but can look plastic on burnished clay. These finishes protect the still-porous clay from handling stains and allow cleaning as needed. Though waterproofed, saggar-fired porcelain should not be used to contain water for longer than eight hours. Also, the surfaces need to be totally protected when transported. Abrasion of any kind can rub away color and finish. Bubble wrap works well.

Refiring pots has been mentioned for a variety of reasons. Changes always result: color can increase, decrease, migrate or transform. Carbon can be cleared from a piece without losing the desirable warm colors by bisque firing it to Cone 07. Refiring a large pot too many times, however, can result in fractures. Saggar-fired pots do not refire well in the range of Cone 10 reduction. But, low-fire glazes have good salvage potential for such pots.

Safety considerations: wear a respirator anytime ceramic fiber is handled and until after fibers settle. The firing cycle can create potentially harmful fumes, so make sure that the kiln room is well ventilated and gases cannot invade occupied areas. Wear a respirator with charcoal acid gas cartridges when tending the firing during its latter stages. If you are trying some of the more exotic compounds, learn what they do at those temperatures, and take appropriate precautions. Risk-taking in all areas, except personal safety, is important to saggar firing if progress is to be made.

One friend shook his head at the uncertainty of the process and said, "If you want color on your pots, why not just put it there to begin with?" For me, it is satisfying and challenging to lavish work on the clay, create interesting surfaces, yet through the firing process, come up with colors contrived. Saggar firing is more about collaborating than dictating. The kiln can be generous or quirky, even vindictive. Those of us who saggar fire have been described as being masochistic. Actually, we are just optimists who are sure the next firing will result in pure magic. ▲

Two high-alumina shelves form the saggar lid; ceramic fiber weighted with posts seals the crack between the shelves.

Cones inside the saggar record rather than monitor firing temperature; color response is best between Cone 012 and 04.

Carbon blackened the exposed areas of a small pot wrapped with wire and tape, then fired in dense wood shavings.

The taller jar reveals patterns from volatile materials influenced but not dominated by masking tape and wire.

Fast Fossils
Carbon-Film Transfer on Saggar-Fired Porcelain

by Dick Lehman

"Torqued Vase," 9 inches in height, thrown and altered porcelain, saggar fired with ferns.

Many years ago I discovered, while doing an American-style raku firing, that fresh leaves and grasses can, under the right conditions, create vegetation images on hot pots: During an all-day firing marathon, a storm blew up unexpectedly. The tornado-force winds arrived so quickly I didn't have time to stop the firing that was in progress. I had just pulled a large bottle out of the kiln, flamed it in sawdust and covered it with a metal garbage can. Fierce gusts of wind unexpectedly blew the trash can half a block away, and the still-thousand-degree bottle rolled down a dirt embankment, through some grasses, and came to rest against a fence post. To say that the retrieval of both the cover and pot was "spirited" would be an understatement—but well worth the effort. After the pot had cooled, I was amazed to see that the copper-stained surface had retained images from the grasses through which it had rolled.

I continued to fire in the waning wind, hoping to possibly replicate the "accident" by placing the very next fresh-from-the-kiln copper-stained pot on its side, atop a mound of sawdust covered with freshly picked sumac leaves. Twenty minutes later, I had my first successful follow-up piece: a lovely, soft likeness of the sumac appeared on the pot. Subsequent firings also yielded successes.

Several years later, however, I abandoned my pursuit of American raku as I had known it, as I was disillusioned by the fading/reoxidizing surfaces of the copper stain. The once-brilliant colors, after several years, became drab and muted, much to my disappointment and that of my customers. It was a hard decision: I loved the vivid images of vegetation against the serendipitous variation of the copper coloring. So I began to look for some other method of firing that might capture that magical blend of spontaneity and explicit detail. Somehow, I intuitively moved toward saggar firing.

Looking back, I realize that it was an unlikely leap of logic that caused me to assume saggar firing would be the answer—that saggar firing would somehow capture the explicit detail of fresh vegetation pressed against pots, while still offering unpredictable, spontaneous surfaces. And it was likely one of those acts of grace or good fortune that occasionally enter each of our lives that caused the startlingly successful results in my first "veggie-saggar" attempt: wonderfully explicit images of vegetation dancing in and through the "celestial" patterning that blessed the rest of the pots' surfaces. I say good fortune, because for the next several hundred firings, there were no successes at all. Oh yes, the pots had some markings, but no explicit plant imagery.

Perhaps it was a healthy state of denial that caused me to keep trying, in the face of relentless failure (surely it will happen again if I just work hard enough). Perhaps it was my life-long interest in landscape photography and my passion for images that were close up, revealing explicit and intimate detail (like those made by Paul Caponigro and Arthur Lazar), that spurred me on. Then again, maybe it was the too-easy transition from tornado-accident to regular successes in the "veggie raku" realm that caused me to remain stubbornly optimistic.

It was an odd and curious experience to see on my desk each day several successful veggie-saggar pieces—pots with delightfully delicate imagery, pots with such explicit detail that I could see the veins and tears and worm holes in many of the leaves, pots that were the ceramic counterparts to the contact prints I routinely made from my 4×5 negatives in the darkroom, pots that had seemed so easy to produce in my first attempt—and at the same time to be continually, perpetually, interminably failing in subsequent attempts to produce any more of them.

Although I continued to experiment with the process, I was not able to explore it in a full-time manner (as I was producing and supervising in a full-time production studio). Over the course of about a year and a half, I tried to reproduce the effect on several hundred pots. Each unsuccessful unloading had me scratching my head, writing more notes about procedural decisions made in that particular firing and comparing the results with the pieces on the desk.

If ever a character defect was an artistic advantage, perhaps in this case my stubbornness was. Unable to believe that I couldn't repeat the results of that first firing, I kept trying. And, eventually, I began to see at least occasional results that lived up to my hopes.

It helped to pay particular attention to several variables: a) sawdust particle size; b) the amount of sawdust in the saggars; c) the type, thickness, substance and placement of the

"Flattened Bottle with Wooden Box," 11 inches in height, wheel-thrown and altered porcelain, saggar fired with sumac and dill weed.

"Torqued Vase," 10 inches in height,
wheel-thrown and altered porcelain,
saggar fired with sumac.

vegetation; d) the firing temperature;
e) the kind of kiln in which the saggar
is fired; f) the kind of saggar used; g)
the manner in which the saggar is
sealed; h) the length of time the saggar is cooled; and i) the manner in
which all of these variables work together. It was only after identifying
these variables that I was able to reproduce what I had stumbled upon
in that first successful firing. However, even now, more than ten years
later, the best results are sparingly attained. With a success rate for the
best works at less than 20%, I've had
to develop a tolerance for more fail-
ures than successes.

Typically, a saggar is partially filled
with 5 inches of fine sawdust. The
pot is laid sideways onto the sawdust
and pressed down to create a "nest."
The pot is removed, and fresh vegetation is positioned in the nest. Then
the pot is put back in place—on its
side atop of the vegetation. Next,
more vegetation is placed onto the
exposed top side of the pot. It is
then covered by an additional 5 inches
of fine sawdust. The saggar is then
closed with a lid.

During the firing, an anaerobic
(no oxygen) atmosphere develops inside the lidded saggar. The vegetation
turns into "activated charcoal" and,
in the process, releases a film of carbon. The bisqued porcelain absorbs
the carbon, capturing the image released by the vegetation.

This speedup process mimics, according to the paleontologists to
whom I have spoken, the much slower
fossil-formation process called "carbonization" or "carbon-film transfer"
(in which volatile materials, such as
nitrogen and oxygen, are squeezed out
of vegetation, and chemical action
changes the tissues of the vegetation
into a thin film of carbon). What remains is residue, forming an outline
of a portion of the leaves. If thick
accumulations of plants derived from
swampy coastal lagoons or deltas are
carbonized more completely, coal deposits may develop.

Because the saggar maintains a relatively anaerobic atmosphere, the

vegetation does not burn (instead, becomes activated charcoal), and is still present after the firing is completed. The anaerobic atmosphere also explains why the carbon image on the pot is not burned away: red-heat temperatures would "perceive" the carbon in the image as a fuel and burn it off the pot if oxygen were present for the combustion process.

Very slight air leaks in the lid of the saggar may cause white areas on the surface of the pot to occur (in these cases, carbon is burned away). Careful control of the particle size and depth of the sawdust can lend a bit of mastery over the light and dark areas—allowing one to dictate whether the carbon images read as "negatives" or "positives," and adding to the sense of the miraculous that sometimes attends results.

Regarding the miraculous: the paleontologists with whom I have spoken have referred to the "miracle" of fossil preservation, due to the vulnerability of organisms to decay and destruction after death (and the resulting potential loss of record of many "individuals" or even entire species). Recently, a combustion chemist visited my studio and expressed a similar perspective regarding the unlikelihood of consistently creating these "fast fossils" (due in large part to the near-endless number of variables at work in "simple" cellulose combustion or partial combustion).

Something about the unlikelihood of this process and its elusiveness is an attraction to me. It is an arena in which there is much to learn: one could choose to take a paleontological or combustion chemistry approach in an attempt to discover what is actually happening, and such research would, no doubt, offer some keys to additional methods of control in what is otherwise a rather capricious process.

Indeed, there is much to master simply through the continued practice of the firing process (regardless of what one understands of the paleontological or combustion-chemistry implications of the

"Bottle with Eared Handles," 8 inches in height, wheel-thrown porcelain, saggar fired with ferns and sumac, by Dick Lehman, Goshen, Indiana.

method). Careful observation and documentation of one's decisions should continue to yield tools that may offer a little more control.

Nonetheless, the inherent lack of control that will always accompany this approach to firing and surface articulation is also what contributes to some of its most amazing successes. I believe the process produces results that are far superior to anything I might achieve, even if I did control most or all of the variables. In that respect, this approach, while full of loss and disappointment, is also full of wonder and surprise—an approach that transforms me into as much a receiver as a producer. It is, in part, this mystery that propels me to continue this work. ▲

Rediscovering The Kiln

Seashell Fuming

by Kelvin Bradford

The challenge of clays, form and firing is a never-ending delight. I started collecting ceramics in the early 1970s and shortly thereafter had my first lessons at Auckland Studio Potters. I was immediately intrigued with the form of vases—particularly Asian-style vases. Then, in the early 1980s, I saw an exhibition of anagama work by Chester Nealie, now a resident in Australia, and was surprised by the looseness of his forms.

Subsequently, I started experimenting with throwing asymmetrical forms. At the same time, the idea of producing natural effects, which to me provide unequalled beauty, acted as a catalyst for seashell fuming experimentation in a gas-fired kiln.

The concept of this fuming method came from Peter Alger, a New Zealand ceramic artist who had already done some firings with seashells, while technical support came from Len Castle, a close friend who made many helpful suggestions.

The Clay Body

Originally, I used a commercial iron-bearing stoneware mixed with grog for strength. I then changed to a white handbuilding clay, naturally grogged, with enormous strength, which is particularly well suited to asymmetrical forms. I had used this white clay exclusively until recent experiments with a Japanese clay, which has extremely high iron content (in the vicinity of 12%), but it is not readily available in New Zealand. The Japanese clay has permitted me to develop a different range of effects, capitalizing on the high iron content.

I have now tested about six iron-bearing clays, but no two reacted entirely the same. Results were dependent on the particular iron content of each clay. For example, the unusual effect created on the piece I

"Midnight," approximately 5 inches in height, wheel-thrown Akatsuchi clay, fired inverted in a saggar filled with oyster shells.

Kelvin Bradford faceting the walls of a loosely thrown vase.

call "Midnight," which was thrown from the iron-rich Japanese clay, was achieved by firing it inverted to increase fuming results. Attempts to reproduce that type of effect with similar clays have not succeeded.

Slips

My slips consist of 80% kaolin and 20% ball clay, the key element being the ball clay, a naturally occurring New Zealand clay that has a very high iron content. Known as "Hyde ball clay," it will produce slightly different results, depending on where in the pit it was mined.

The slips are applied to the pots when they are leather hard. The best

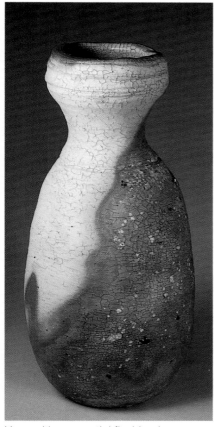

Vase with sequential flashing in a
rainbowlike band, approximately
18 inches in height.

Wheel-thrown stoneware vase with kaolin slip, approximately 7 inches in height,
fumed with rock oyster shells.

results are obtained if they are brushed on rather than dipped. I tend to build up several layers of slip over a period of two days.

The Saggar

I have tried loading the kiln in a number of different ways with differently sized saggars, and now have a permanent saggar that occupies 80% of the kiln. The base consists of two large shelves, which have been cut around the burners to maximize kiln space, and a 1.27 centimeter gap in the center. This gap is maintained throughout two additional chambers, each constructed with a 0.5 centimeter gap for breathing at the top.

Changing the size of the saggar will affect the fuming time and results. Of course the lighter the saggar, the faster one can fire. It is also possible to construct minisaggars within the three-chamber situation, which I have often done. However, it is essential to keep variables to a minimum in a controlled situation.

The earliest experiments were carried out utilizing bisqued pots fumed in shells to 1050°C (1922°F). These pots were then taken out of the saggar, placed in the kiln with an ordinary glaze firing and refired in oxidation to 1280°C (2336°F). This produced unusual effects, inevitably quiet with an absence of bright color.

Then instead of fuming to 1050°C and refiring to 1280°C, I decided to fire straight through. At this stage, I was still firing in oxidation. But in one firing, I obtained brilliant flashing of color, and after some pondering, decided that perhaps there had been some reduction in the firing within the saggar. By reducing from 1000°C until 1280°C in the next firing, I produced some outstanding red flashes. From that time on, I have always reduced heavily from 1000°C to the end of the firing.

Seashells

I have tried a variety of shells, but the rock oyster seems to produce the best "flashing" shell; it will yield vivid red flashings. Using just the flanges of the rock oyster, which are much thinner, will produce yellow flashings, almost white. The mussel shell will produce more muted orange flashings. Crushed smaller shells will produce pastel brown tones and sometimes a very unusual white splatter.

With dry shells (dried in the sun for a week), the tonings will be softer. I found that very old collected shells would not fume at all; however, I was able to utilize old seashells to obtain a ghosting effect. Conversely, if the shells are soaked in salt water, a different range of effects may be created, including heavy salt encrustation.

I usually collect shells within two hours either side of high water and will quickly wash them, as (particularly with the oyster shells) it is possible for mud or sand to be trapped inside. These will leave undesirable heavy black streaks on the pieces.

Loading and Firing

For a long time, I have preset the pots on pads in the saggar. It is easier to plan what effects may be attempted when one first decides which pots are going to be fired. Please note, I always wear a mask and gloves when loading or unloading the kiln.

With preset planning, the only problem that I have encountered is positioning shells near the central air space. It is difficult to prevent them from actually falling through the air space. However, it is surprising how one can improvise and support shells as they are positioned around the pieces and built up in layers.

Loading may take up to three hours, even for a medium-sized gas kiln, and is entirely dependent upon the number of pots being fired and the effects I am trying to achieve.

Very often the shells are wet, therefore it is risky to immediately commence firing. My kilns have electric heaters and I usually preheat overnight to 150°C (302°F).

Vase, approximately 7 inches in height, iron-rich stoneware with kaolin slip, fired inverted to 1280°C (2336°F).

Seashell-fumed vase, approximately 16 inches in height, by Kelvin Bradford, Warkworth, New Zealand.

Rock oyster shells are gathered within two hours of high tide, then washed to remove unwanted sand and mud.

Firing takes seven to ten hours. Between 450°C (842°F) and 600°C (1112°F), the shells will sometimes audibly "crack." The recommended peak temperature is 1250°–1290°C (2282°–2354°F) with a one-hour soak. Just above 1290°C, "texture" is created, and it will change into a glaze and even run, which is undesirable.

Refiring is possible but the results are somewhat unpredictable. I only attempt it if, for example, one side of a piece is completely bland or there is insufficient color. When refiring, I place a minimum of shells where there is an absence of color.

The Fuming Sequence

Most shells will not flash above their own height. The exception is the rock oyster shell, which will fume up to 1.27 centimeters when placed against a piece. The necks of pieces without flashing can be unattractive; to avoid this, shells must be packed up to the rim, or the piece placed as close as 1.27 centimeters to the top of the saggar, which will reflect down and give reverse flashing. It is also possible to suspend shells within the neck to create additional color. In order to increase the fuming effects at the top of a piece, I will fire it inverted. The results obtained are often extremely powerful and sometimes gaps must be left in order for colors to break, saving monotony or overpowering effects.

There appears to be a definite sequence of flashing. I did not realize this until I started experimenting with breaking up overpowering flashing effects. The first stage is red where the shells are thin, then there is a sequential change of colors in a rainbowlike band that can be up to 2.54 centimeters wide.

I find being able to create colors like these using natural seashells in a gas kiln extraordinary, and plan to continue to experiment with saggar fuming techniques to achieve a range of effects. ▲

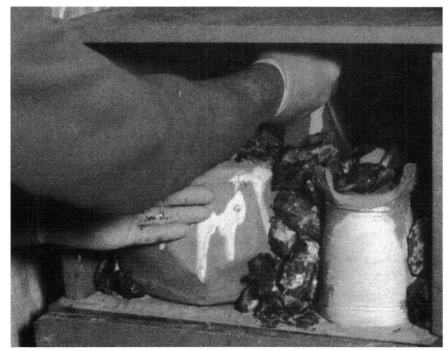

The shells are carefully positioned in and around the pots, building up in layers to avoid having any fall through the central air space.

David Atamanchuk

by Joel Perron

Graceful, quiet and technically refined to the point of mystery, the work of David Atamanchuk, raises many questions—both explicit and implicit. But, according to Atamanchuk, a Canadian studying pottery in one form or another for some 15 years in Japan, there's one question that is always asked: "How can a foreigner make such Japanese pots?"

So what's so Japanese about them? Perhaps it is the earthy colors, classically Asian shapes, or subtle balance of function with beauty.

Besides a steady marketplace—as evidenced by the fact that 90% of his customers are Japanese—Japan also offers Atamanchuk the opportunities he seeks to visit some of the world's most remarkable museum collections of Asian ceramics. It was at Idemitsu Museum of Art in Tokyo where in 1979 he began an in-depth study of everything from ancient Persian to Chinese and Japanese wares, from complete pots down to mere shards. After two years, he was allowed to actually handle virtually any of the museum's pieces. He followed his study at Idemitsu with more ceramic research at the Tokyo University of Fine Arts in 1983.

Undoubtedly, such a thorough academic grounding is what gives Atamanchuk's pots their sturdy Asian classicism, whether the vessel be a flower vase, incense burner, teabowl or sake cup. But, there is more to his work than untiring emulation of Asian models. Some casual observers may overlook the contemporary flavor of his interpretations. The fact that he melds aesthetics spanning millennia reflects a certain necessary distance from tradition— bending it to his individual purpose.

Walking through the lustered porcelain vessels, earthy saggar-fired vases and crackle-glazed raku incense burners, one starts to get a sense of his persevering experimental nature and the flexibility that goes with it.

Wheel-thrown vase, approximately 15 inches in height, Shigaraki clay fired in a saggar surrounded by sawdust, copper sulfate and a small amount of salt.

The wisps of white floating across scorched, unglazed vases, for example, are an effect of firing with salt put into individual containers within the pots— a technique more limited and controlled than throwing salt into the kiln during the firing.

Another technique involves the use of sawdust and copper sulfide in saggar firings. The resulting patterns are to a large extent unpredictable but Atamanchuk can anticipate some red areas due to reduction.

Incorporating his initials as a conspicuous design element is another practice setting Atamanchuk apart from traditional discretion in Japanese ceramics. It also signifies his desire for individuality and in this sense reflects an unabashed modernity. ▲

"Yakishime Vase," approximately 18 inches in height, wheel-thrown Shigaraki clay, fired in a saggar surrounded by sawdust and copper sulfate to 1250°C (2282°F).

Saggar-fired vase, approximately 11 inches in height, wheel-thrown Shigaraki clay, by David Atamanchuk, Atami-Shi, Shizuoka-Ken, Japan.

Rediscovering The Kiln

Elisabeth Anderson

by Virginia Hillhouse

On a recent trip to New Mexico, my first stop was in front of a sawdust-smoked pot by Elisabeth Anderson. Its classical form intentionally askew, the bowl was standing alone in a case at the Albuquerque International Airport. The colors echoed the gray-green and sand shades of the land, and the pink hues of the adobe homes and nearby Sangre de Cristo mountains.

Determined to meet the artist, I launched an informal, if circuitous, search and found her at home. Anderson discusses her pots with the fervor of an explorer on the brink of discovering new territory; the unknown fuels her enthusiasm. Experiments and modifications in raku firing give a protean quality to her work.

Trained in the sciences (her major was anthropology), she is a self-taught potter, though self-teaching better describes her continual quest. Any formal ceramics education has been in workshops, primarily at Colorado's Anderson Ranch.

"I began my career in clay as a collector," Anderson recalled. And, indeed, for the first 10 years of the more than 30 that she has been active in the pottery world, she never made a pot.

In 1962, Anderson moved with her husband and three children to Hiroshima; she admits now that she was not prepared for the impact of Japanese culture. "I became enmeshed in the environment, living in a Japanese house and learning the language." However, it was when friends took her to see the mingei or folk-craft artists that she was truly hooked on pottery.

"In Mashiko (100 miles north of Tokyo) at the magnificent compound of Shoji Hamada, we watched as Hamada's son removed his father's pieces from the kiln. He allowed us to select whatever object we wanted, and I chose two teacups with a bamboo design, the bamboo seeming to blow in the wind."

Anderson also discovered Kyushu, one of Japan's southern islands, where pottery making is still a way of life for the descendants of Koreans who settled there in the 16th century. In the traditional mingei way, Kyushu potters work communally, none receiving recognition over another. Anderson admired the asymmetry and strong shapes of their pots, adding several to her collection.

A few years later, a sabbatical took the family to Australia, where "out of sheer boredom, I decided to take a clay workshop," recalled Anderson. "From then on, I never let go." Once back in Albuquerque, she acquired her own pottery equipment.

Anderson's most successful pieces are the result of her propensity to experiment. A survey of her tools—salad spoons, paddles, garbage can lid, paper towels, table salt—suggests that home has been her best laboratory.

"I begin by cutting, with my garbage can lid as a guide, two disks of Cone 10 sculpture clay," explained Anderson. She then puts the two pieces together with shredded newspaper stuffed inside, seals the edges, wraps the entire piece in plastic and suspends it in a sling above the worktable. At this point, she may texture the clay with a piece of lava.

The following day, she opens the pot, removes its paper contents and begins shaping—this is when the salad spoons ("they have nice curves") and big, sturdy paddles from a cookware store come into play. Then, using a sand-filled sock, she pushes, flattens and contours the surface. Sometimes, the final touch before leaving the pot to harden is attaching the neck, a cylinder thrown on the wheel. A bisque firing follows.

Living in the southwest, Anderson has felt the strong presence of Native American pottery, and once tried burnishing smaller pots with a stone as her pueblo counterparts do. But "after five minutes, it was drudgery," she noted. Consequently, she found her own way—coating each pot with lots of slip, then rubbing it with a paper towel for 20–30 minutes. "It gives a wet look, like river rocks under water. In the finished pot, I strive to recreate the soft, satin sheen of a wet pot."

To ready the pot for final firing, she may cover the surface with table salt (adhered with wax resist). Or she may add designs with randomly wrapped wire or torn paper towels dipped in clay slip. Then comes the stage that gives her

Above: Sawdust-fired vessel with forged silver, 13 inches in diameter, Cone 10 sculpture clay, with burnished slip and table salt (in wax resist).

Right: Slab-built pot, 20 inches in diameter, wrapped with paper towels dipped in slip, coated with table salt, filled with damp sawdust (from a horse stall), then fired between 1200°F and 1800°F.

Rediscovering The Kiln

Low-fire-salt vase, 22 inches in height, slab built, slipped and burnished, wrapped with wire, filled with damp sawdust.

Vase with copper wire, 21 inches in height, sculpture clay with burnished slip and table salt, filled with sawdust, low fired.

Slab-built bowl with burnished slip and salt, 18 inches wide, sawdust smoked, by Elisabeth Anderson, Albuquerque, New Mexico.

pots their subtle colors. Each is filled with damp, used sawdust (shoveled from a neighbor's horse stall), and fired between 1200°F and 1800°F. "It varies because I'm terrible about peeking," she admitted. The pot is removed only when cool enough to handle. Half the sawdust will have burned; the rest is ash.

Her kiln resembles a 2-foot cube. (However, she can add rows of bricks to the top for larger pots.) There is a hinged door—good for easy removal as well as peeking. "I seem to have the best luck with this size," she said, "but I am still learning the secrets of this kiln and how to take advantage of them."

Anderson's method of smoking was "developed accidentally. I can't claim an invention," she insisted. Commissioned several years ago to make a number of large pots, Anderson realized there was no way she could physically lift the red-hot pots from the kiln for postfiring reduction. So she took the risk of trying a one-step procedure with the combustible sawdust inside instead of outside the pot. "The first time I tried, I was blown away by the colors. I have continued to develop and refine this firing technique," she said, "but I fancy the horse urine is the magic potion.

"Experimenting is what keeps me going," observed Anderson. Sometimes her experiments include working with other artists.

A friendship begun in Australia between Anderson and Pamela Warner, who works in hand-forged sterling silver, has continued in the U.S. since 1978. "Gluing the silver onto a pot that is not round calls for lots of hand fitting and hard work, but it only enhances the piece," said Anderson, who gives Warner total freedom.

Anderson's daughter-in-law Diane Egbert, a California jeweler, also adds metal (copper or bronze wire) to her pots. "The binding with wire adds to the tension I am creating and the copper reminds me of the veins that run through rocks," explained Anderson.

In addition to her sculptural pots, Anderson is currently making wall pieces. They too reflect the rock formations and natural shapes that she admires. "Pieces I am doing now look more and more like rocks. It is ironic and amusing to me that I'm taking clay (originally rock) and putting it back in its original shape." ▲

Working with a Cone 10 sculpture clay, Anderson begins by rolling out a slab on top of a cloth sling, then uses a garbage can lid as a guide to cut out a disk. Still on the cloth, the disk is gently shaped in a slump mold. A second disk is attached along the edges to the first, with the hollow between them stuffed with shredded newspaper. The next day, the newspaper is removed, and the pot is shaped by paddling with wooden spoons and a sand-filled sock.

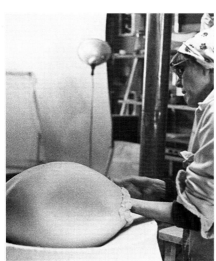

Smokeless Saggar Firings

by Macy Dorf

Since 1968, I have been making pottery as a full-time profession. While exploring and refining my functional line, I have always had a nagging desire to make one-of-a-kind decorative work as well. After many years of experimenting with different forms and techniques, I became intrigued with the process of sawdust firing in saggars. And that has introduced new directions with challenging new problems.

Here in Denver, Colorado, we have a problem with smog during the winter months. In an attempt to cut down on atmospheric emissions, city councils throughout the metropolitan area have disallowed wood burning on high-pollution days. Firing sawdust saggars on those days placed me in violation of these local ordinances.

Although I arranged my firing schedule so that combustion occurred around midnight, when the smog problem is at its lowest, a conscientious passerby once saw my kiln's smoke late at night and notified the fire department. When the firemen arrived, I was called to the studio—a 12-mile drive—to discuss the situation. Their suggestion was to change my firing schedule so that the heaviest smoke occurred in the early morning hours, closer to daylight.

Some time after making this adjustment, I began receiving angry complaints from my upstairs neighbor informing me that the smoke smell in his studio was unbearable on certain mornings. My alternatives were to stop sawdust firing, move to another city or country (my neighbor preferred the latter), or do something to fix the problem. Naturally, my preference was to fix it—and fast. After spending a few sleepless nights worrying, I came up with the idea of inserting a catalytic-type chamber into the flue to burn off the smoke before it reached the atmosphere.

With some advice, I proceeded to make several chimney alterations. The first was to increase the height of the kiln stack from 10 feet to 30 feet. Then, between the floor and

An added burner at the base of the chimney plus a much taller stack eliminate smoke from saggar firings.

damper, I added a new burner with the flame directed into the flue. This inexpensive burner, made by Gas Appliance Company, has a Btu range of 17,490 to 78,440 (I use approximately 6 inches of water column pressure, which gives me 68,000 BTUs).

Also, I installed a large industrial pilot because the flue draft had been pulling the flames from the smaller pilots. This large pilot was made by Killam Gas Burner Company and, at 6-inch pressure, has 4600 BTUs.

I leave the added burner on until the flue gets to red heat. Then, because at this point the kiln is burning off all emissions, I turn it off and plug up the hole.

For that first firing after the adjustments, I started a normal firing in the late afternoon. When I returned to the studio the next morning, I was disheartened to find everything smelling of smoke—including the work area of my upstairs neighbor! However, on close inspection, I was relieved to see that the damper was pushed in too far, causing the smoke to seep out of the peeps and around the door rather than through the heated flue. Fortunately, all I needed to do was open the damper to draw the smoke up the flue where it could be burned off in a less offensive manner.

Escaping smoke has since been eliminated from my saggar firings. My upstairs neighbor has been completely unaware of my firing schedule, and I can now save gas by starting a firing in the morning, avoiding the overnight soak. Last spring a Cinco de Mayo celebration brought 20,000 people to my studio's neighborhood and not one person complained of either smoke or the smell of my firing saggar.

With these problems behind me, I can only hope that the next one waits a while to crop up. The studio is back to being a working space rather than a construction zone, my upstairs neighbor is appeased, and I am now firing saggars in an environmentally better manner. ▲

RETURNING TO THE ROOTS:
Burnishing and black firing

One of the most seductive of clay surfaces is that of the highly burnished blackware typical of the work of some Pueblo Indian potters. A well-burnished pot has a surface as reflective as that of a glossy glaze, but with a glow that seems to come from within the clay itself. To glaze a pot is to coat it with glass, but to burnish it is to rearrange the clay particles themselves to produce a smooth surface. Natural clay color is attractive enough burnished—but blackening a burnished pot seems to make it glossier. Though many of the artists profiled thus far burnish their work to some degree, a completely blackened pot is most successful if it has been burnished to the highest possible sheen. Therefore, the artists in this chapter describe their burnishing methods in some detail.

"Black firing" can be accomplished in a variety of ways. The key is somehow to smother the fire when the fuel is burning well, creating a lot of smoke around the pots. This can be accomplished by means of a raku-like technique, heating a pot in a kiln and then placing the hot pot into a barrel filled with newspaper and covering it. However, burnished pottery is usually made from a smooth clay, which might not stand up to such a treatment and, furthermore, the polished surface is delicate and could be scratched if the pot is picked up with tongs. Thus, it is preferable to use methods such as firing in a saggar or barrel, or to fire in the Pueblo manner.

Though Pueblo potters fire in a variety of ways, one typical Pueblo method of blackening pots is to stack them over, but not directly on, the fuel surrounded and protected by metal grates, bedsprings, license plates, or pottery shards. This whole stack may then be covered with more fuel—typically dried cow dung—and lighted. When the fire has attained sufficient heat, it may be smothered with soil to retain the smoke against the pots. Interestingly, though this firing technique is thought of as "traditional," it is a relatively new tradition reinvented this century by potter Maria Martinez in an effort to duplicate black shards found at archaeological sites.

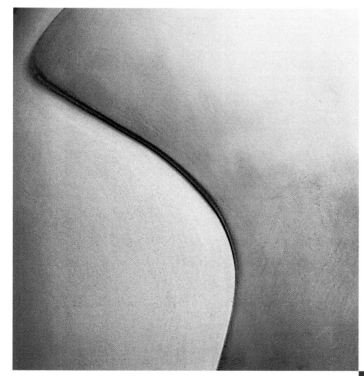

Juan Quezada
Potter in a New Tradition
by Elaine Levin

Above right: Juan Quezada mines clay near his home in Mata Ortiz, Mexico. A self-taught potter, Juan established a repertoire of bodies, pigments and slips by trial-and-error experimentation with local materials.

Opposite page: Handbuilt jar with polychrome slip decoration, approximately 7 inches in diameter, by Juan Quezada.

Below: Laying down an overall pattern in black pigment, Juan demonstrates this initial step in his decorative process.

Pottery collectors would understand Spencer MacCallum's excitement when he stumbled on some jars that resembled old Casas Grandes ware while on a business trip in southern New Mexico in 1976. Impelled by his anthropologist's training to explore a local junk shop, Spencer's curiosity was aroused when the owner insisted the jars were not old but had been traded by poor people from Mexico for used clothing. The jars' complex patterns and maze-like lines were compelling and led him to search northern Mexico to find the potter. Armed only with photos of the pots (to eliminate problems with customs), Spencer questioned everyone he met. He was finally directed to a small village south of the ancient Casas Grandes capital of Paquimé. Since Pueblo Indian potters are traditionally female, Spencer was skeptical when Juan Quezada, a former woodcutter and railroad laborer, claimed the ware. Juan was amazed that anyone would search the countryside for his pottery, commenting that the junk shop specimens did not even represent his best efforts.

This concern for quality, Spencer later learned, was characteristic of Juan who, at 39, continues to search for ways to improve his shapes, colors and designs. Entirely self-taught, Juan was attracted to clay by the potsherds he found working as a woodcutter at age 13 in the mountains above his village. These fragments of Casas Grandes culture excited his imagination in the same way Nampeyo (Tewa potter of the Hopi First Mesa) and Maria and Julian Martinez of San Ildefonso were inspired by potsherds found in excavations of ruins near their homes. Unlike these famous potters, Juan had no family tradition from which to acquire skills. As a youngster he would draw on any available surfaces, experimenting to make paints from whatever natural materials he

could find, even grasshoppers. Later, he gathered materials for colorants and slips while working in the mountains where at times he collected wild honey, acorns and maguey shoots to supplement the living he earned cutting firewood. Juan saved the potsherds he found, breaking and examining them again and again, finally reasoning, at age 15, that he could make pottery too because the materials to produce such ware must be all around him. At first, the technology escaped him. He would give it up, then return again to struggle with the clay. The first successful jars he gave away to friends, and soon traders from Palomas and Casas Grandes came to buy. The idea of doing something enjoyable while earning a living had not occurred to him until the first sale.

Spencer and Juan met some six years later and, by that time, Juan had developed his own procedures with clay. Not far from his village he found several different kinds of clay, some containing a natural fine sand temper. By blending these, he developed a formula that has yielded good plasticity, firing strength and a warm color. After the body has aged two to three weeks, he extracts a ball of it, forming a tortilla shape, evening the thickness with a rolling pin. This he lays in a bowl-like mold, trimming away excess, smoothing with his fingers. The plaster form gives the pot a rounded bottom and resembles clay molds used by prehistoric potters— something Juan did not know until he and his brother Nicolas later chanced upon some in a mountain cave. A single, thick coil of clay is added to the bottom slab, around the edge of the bowl, its thickness determined by the jar's intended size. With edges firmly attached, the vessel is slowly turned, the walls thinned and moved upward as Juan's fingers pinch it evenly to ⅛-inch thick. With regular motions

of a rasp knife edge on the outside against finger pressure from within, he obtains a uniform wall, using a regular knife blade to prepare the surface for slip and painting.

Before a pot dries, a cream of light beige slip is applied. When that is firm, Juan begins a design, working intuitively, with no prescribed pattern, making each vessel's decoration differently, although certain elements—parts of animals, hatched lines, steps and checkerboards—appear in altered combinations on many of the jars. Laying black lines first, he turns the pot 180 degrees as each is completed so that the symmetrical repetition of units will be as exact as possible. While repetition also characterizes Casas Grandes Ramos polychrome ware, Juan's vessels display a more complex, interlocking progression. Solid color areas of black pigment are filled in first, then the red areas and finally the black outlining the red areas is repainted to make the boundaries sharp and clear. Vegetable oil is dabbled on the surface of the jar to impede overly rapid drying that would cause the clay to split. The only nod to Western technology is a piece of plastic film applied over the jar as he lightly and rapidly rubs it with a stone to seat the colors. Juan conjectures that his Casas Grandes predecessors used the thin skin of the maguey plant for the same purpose as he has done experimentally. The jar is set aside to dry enough for the actual burnishing; one of the best stones for this purpose is chalcedony, which is shaped by abrasion under water, then polished with leather. After burnishing, the pot is dried for several days before firing.

Some time after Juan began to actively work with clay, his mother mentioned that her mother had been a potter, learning the art from Juan's great-grandmother. The tradition was broken during his mother's childhood when enamelware

1–4 Juan handbuilds pots by first laying a tortilla-shaped slab in a concave plaster mold, then adding a series of pinched coils. Walls are evened with a rasp knife and opposing finger pressure; smoothing with a regular knife blade prepares the surface for polychrome slip decoration.

Right: Handbuilt earthenware jar, 9 inches in diameter, constructed of smoothed, pinched coils; slip decorated, dung fired, by Juan Quezada.

Below right: Earthenware jar, 8 inches in diameter, polychrome slip decoration, dung fired.

became popular and the market for pottery declined; consequently, Juan's mother could offer no technical advice. Juan learned to fire by trial and error, first with wood, then charcoal and finally with dried cow chips. With the latter, his procedures resemble those of the Southwest Indians, as he protects his jars from direct flame by placing each one under an inverted bucket, elevated slightly on stones so that hot air will circulate. The dung is piled up around the bucket and braced in place by stiff wires, doused with kerosene and ignited. Fifteen or twenty minutes of burning is usually sufficient and the pot is removed to cool in the house oven.

By 1976, although Juan had perfected the basic pottery skills, he was not satisfied with the work—with seven children and a wife to support, he could not devote enough time to develop further. Spencer felt he could best help Juan toward his artistic goals by offering a fixed amount of money each month in exchange for his pottery, with no stipulation that he must produce a certain amount or kind of work. The arrangement (agreed upon after Spencer had made several trips to Mata Ortiz) has allowed Juan to experiment with new materials and firing techniques. A recent change in his ware occurred after a visit to relatives some distance from his village. An elderly resident identified a large olla—used for making *tesquino*, a fermented corn drink—as one made by Juan's great-grandmother. The size of the jar and the relationship to the potter inspired Juan to work beyond his usual 6- to 8-inch-high jars. He has since produced vessels 16 to 18 inches in height, changing his patterns for the larger contoured space.

Not restrained by the past, Juan had begun to paint the bottoms of his pots, gradually eliminating the "equator" just below the jar's belly. In prehistoric times, this line was drawn above the mold which secured the vessel's base, and the jar was not painted beneath it. Without this boundary the surface opens to a larger motif, allowing curvilinear lines to sweep across the rounded bottom.

Diagonal lines, one of the dominant motifs in Juan's designs, define the panels on the pot's surface as well as creating negative *caminos* (paths) that can be traced around the vessel. This maze-like structure is in simpler form on prehistoric ware and appears to be a part of the architecture of ancient Paquimé.

In the last several years, Mata Ortiz has become a pottery center. When Juan began selling his forms, he encouraged family members and villagers, especially the unemployed, to learn pottery skills. Two of his brothers and three sisters, as well as several villagers, became his students. Stressing craftsmanship, Juan has been able to exercise quality control by sharing colors (the ingredients and proportions are his secret) only with those who produce fine ware. Seven households now support themselves with pottery that exhibits styles apart from that of their teacher. The Mexican government has helped the villagers form a cooperative society of potters and find marketing outlets. Spencer MacCallum has gradually introduced Mata Ortiz pottery to others in the Southwest. According to J. R. Pahl, director of the Rex E. Wignal Museum at Chaffey College in Alta Loma, California, Juan Quezada and the potters of Mata Ortiz have brought about the "spontaneous revival of one of the most beautiful traditions in the history of ceramic art." Pahl saw the accomplishments of an original, natural artist as especially important to an area with a large population of Mexican descent, and initiated a five-museum tour of Juan's ware, as well as that of the other leading potters of Mata Ortiz. As Spencer MacCallum wrote in a catalog statement, Juan Quezada's "rediscovery of ceramic technology entirely by experiment . . . stands high as an intellectual accomplishment. As a technological innovator, as an artist and as a teacher, Juan has contributed to the life of his village and to the beauty of the world."

Returning To The Roots

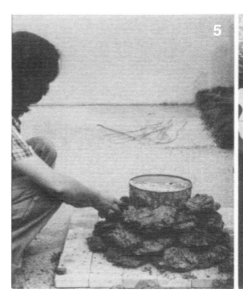

5–7 Juan's sister Lydia and brother Nicolas demonstrate Mata Ortiz firing methods: a thoroughly dry, prewarmed pot is placed on three small stones and covered with an inverted bucket (also elevated on stones to allow the air circulation necessary for an oxidizing atmosphere). Dried cow manure is piled over all, held in place with wires and ignited with the aid of kerosene.

Below: Effigy jar, 9 inches in length, handbuilt with pinched coils, slip decorated, burnished, dung fired.

Right: Several fuels and methods of firing were attempted before Juan arrived at a final solution. Wood produced first clouding; charcoal was slightly better. The ideal fuel proved to be cow dung from grass-fed cows; it must be completely dry to burn cleanly.

8–10 After 15–20 minutes of burning, the supports are removed and the remains of the fire are scattered. With the aid of a sturdy wire, Lydia Quezada lifts the bucket and moves the pot to a location where it can cool slowly. Juan encourages family members and others in his village to learn pottery skills; stressing craftsmanship, he exercises quality control by sharing colors only with those who produce fine ware.

Right: Earthenware jar, 7 inches in height, decorated with polychrome slips, burnished, dung fired.

Below: Earthenware jar, 9 inches in height, handbuilt with pinched coils, slip decorated, burnished, dung fired.

Below right: Handbuilt jar, 7 inches in height, slip decorated, burnished, dung fired, by Juan Quezada.

Returning To The Roots

Burnished pots, two with polychrome slips and one with graphite, to 11 inches in height, by Michael Wisner.

The Spirit to Learn, the Spirit to Teach

by Norbert Turek

Juan Quezada is the internationally known patriarch of a pottery revolution that has revitalized the village of Juan Mata Ortiz in northern Chihuahua, Mexico (see "Juan Quezada" in the September 1980 CM and "Working with Juan Quezada" in the April 1997 CM). In addition to his discoveries directly related to materials and techniques for building, burnishing, decorating and firing pots, Quezada's love of teaching has had such a significant impact that fully one-quarter of the village's residents are now producing decorated ceramics. Quezada has also taught numerous courses in the United States. It was at such a course in California that Michael Wisner, a young potter who had also worked with other renowned Southwestern artists, such as Blue Corn, Lucy Lewis, Fawn Navase and Laura Gachapine, realized they "shared a passion for experimentation and discovery with clay and techniques." For the last ten years, their friendship has been renewed by Wisner's annual pilgrimage to Mata Ortiz, where he works

and studies with Quezada for two to three months. In the spirit of information sharing, Quezada has encouraged Wisner to teach these techniques to his U.S. students.

Over the years, Wisner has adapted Quezada's forming and decorating methods to commercially available ceramics products, and subsequently has taught these modified methods at Anderson Ranch Arts Center in Snowmass Village, Colorado, where he is a resident artist. The students are often amazed at the simplicity with which high-gloss burnished pots are produced. Usually, the classes run only four to five days. Yet, by the end of a course, each student has produced an armful of coil-built, shiny black pots. In between classes, Wisner hunts the Elk Mountains for clay veins that might produce unique results—much as Quezada still wanders his surroundings in search of new materials.

Wisner isn't interested in sharing Southwestern pottery-making ideas just to have more people making Southwestern pots, though. "Part of my

passion and excitement is watching this art form evolve in the hands of sculptors, wheel throwers and handbuilders," he acknowledges. "Seeing how these rich surfaces may be used in the modern art arena is awesome."

He also experiments with techniques that veer away from his teacher's; for example, a gas-firing method that can more safely produce pots as richly black as traditional open bonfires; and a slip-casting body, developed with Montana ceramist Richard Notkin, that will withstand the pressure of burnishing tools.

Finding the Right Body

"At first, I was frustrated because I would return to the U.S. (from Mata Ortiz) only to find commercial clays unsuitable for this style," says Wisner. But "Juan's passion for experimentation kept me going." After several years, he came across a commercial clay that worked—CT-3 from Mile Hi Ceramics in Denver, Colorado. A plastic talc/ball clay body that achieves considerable strength in open-air bonfire firings between 1300°F and 1500°F, it

The bone-dry pot is carefully sanded, then covered with baby oil.

"allows me to burnish to a highly reflective shine with moist clay right out of the bag."

While CT-3 clay works well, Wisner kept looking for a clay body that would fire at a lower temperature. He found that a 50:50 talc/ball body with 2–5% bentonite can yield excellent results. "I know the rule is 2%," says Wisner, "but 5% bentonite works fine, and adds considerable strength to the clay body." He calls this clay body recipe "Mike's Mud," and admits that it takes a little more work to produce than out-of-the-bag commercial clay, but the results are well worth the effort.

Wisner has tried many pot-forming techniques to see how each fares in the stressful bonfire process. Ironically, everything works—including hand-built, wheel-thrown, slab-built and slip-cast pieces. Notkin believes slip-cast objects may actually have an advantage in that the clay has no "particle memory." They also have uniform wall thickness, which promotes even heating.

Preparing the Surface

"It is helpful for the artist to think of burnishing as preparing a canvas for painting. A well-prepared canvas will be smooth, allowing the paintbrush to glide uninterrupted over the surface," says Wisner. For years, he used clay slips as a way to achieve a smooth surface.

Evenly rubbed over the entire surface, the baby oil is allowed to soak in.

Rubbing in a circular motion with a damp cotton T-shirt fills small scratches and smooths irregularities.

After the surface is rubbed again with the damp cloth, the pot is attacked with a burnishing tool.

Returning To The Roots

After seeing Quezada's burnishing technique, Wisner gave up slips because of their limitations. "Slips leave evidence of their application whether done by brushing, dipping or spraying," he says. "They also sometimes flake off when polished or crack when dried. This is not to say that slips don't yield a beautiful surface. But if it's a smooth and shiny surface you're after, nothing beats a fine clay body that has the capacity to be burnished."

The surface must be prepared for burnishing by a series of sandings at the bone-dry stage. First, Wisner uses 100-grit paper to remove any lumps and depressions left from handbuilding or the ridges left from wheel throwing. A little time invested in smoothing the pot while it's wet can save a lot of sanding time. Once the pot is evenly sanded with 100 grit, 220 grit is used to further refine the surface; 220-grit sandpaper erases the coarse tracks left by the 100-grit paper.

The most effective burnishing is achieved by moistening the bone-dry clay surface. Waiting for a pot to reach the right leather-hard state can be very tricky. A dry pot is virtually impossible to burnish, while a very wet pot that is burnished will lose its shine as it dries.

The story is told that everyone in Mata Ortiz used to work on the pots while they were leather hard. If a pot dried out, it had to be discarded. One day Juan Quezada's brother, Reynaldo, made a group of pots and left them covered with a cloth while he attended a nearby festival. Having perhaps enjoyed himself too much, Reynaldo didn't start work until late that next day. To his horror, he saw that the wind had uncovered his pots, and they were all bone dry. In an attempt to salvage his work, Reynaldo rubbed a mixture of oil and water on the bone-dry clay. To his surprise, it actually yielded a finer polishing surface than leather-hard clay. That happy accident completely changed the way pots were burnished in Mata Ortiz.

Michael Wisner's modification of Reynaldo's technique involves the use

For blackware, a graphite slurry is evenly applied with a 2½-inch-wide sponge brush to the entire surface.

After drying 1–2 minutes, the excess graphite is removed by gently rubbing the entire pot with a dry cotton cloth.

For a mirror shine, the surface is burnished in one direction, connecting every stroke, then burnished at a 90° angle to the original strokes.

of baby oil and a damp cloth (the festival is optional). A sanded pot is covered with baby oil and allowed to dry a minute or two until the oil soaks into the clay. Then, a soft cotton cloth (such as a T-shirt) is wetted and wrung out. The damp cloth is rubbed lightly in a circular motion on the clay surface. This removes small scratches in the clay and fills in small irregularities. Two or three wipes are usually sufficient. Too much time on one spot or too much water, and the clay will become too wet.

Next, the pot is rubbed again with the damp T-shirt, this time going over the surface only once and being careful to work across the "rib" of the shirt (rubbing parallel to the rib of the fabric will leave visible lines). This eliminates the fine circular pattern left from the previous step, and leaves the pot extremely smooth and still slightly damp. The surface is now attacked with a burnishing tool.

Putting on a Shine

Wisner first makes all the burnishing strokes in one direction. After going over the entire piece, he returns and burnishes at a 90° angle to the first strokes. This enhances the shine and yields a flawless canvas that the paintbrush can effortlessly glide across.

His burnishing tool of choice is a 12-inch-long, stainless-steel automotive valve push-rod. "It polishes like no other tool I've ever come across," he remarks. "It lays down the surface completely smooth and regular with no small ripples, as you often see with a stone-burnished pot."

But all burnishing tools have their place—spoons, rocks, bones, chamois, even beans. Wisner recommends that all serious pot-shiners keep an array of them in their toolboxes. The diversity gives more options for stubborn clays or radical angles. Successful burnishing requires that the artist be aware of which tool is most effective at any given time. This can vary within minutes on the same pot.

Generally, Wisner does the initial burnish with the steel push-rod. Later, as the surface begins to dry, the steel rod can leave streaks. He may then switch to a polished deer bone or stone to finish the job. Another option is

Materials for a bonfiring: metal bucket, sawdust, manure, firewood, vapor barrier, baling wire, lighter fluid and matches.

Preheated pots are carried from the oven to the firing site wrapped in cotton towels, then placed carefully on firing stands.

skin polishing, which leaves a satin finish, as seen on many oxidized (white- or red-colored) painted pots. "Put away the stones and roll up your sleeves," says Wisner. "I've found the soft skin on the underside of the forearm is a fantastic burnishing tool for satin finishes." Silk scarves or women's fine-mesh stockings are also fine tools for a satin burnish.

Slippery, but Not a Slip

Burnishing a thin coating of ground graphite is new to the American ceramics scene. This user-friendly technique yields a surface with a silvery, gunmetal finish—sometimes so metallic it's easy to mistake the piece for metal.

The graphite "slip" technique was developed in another part of the village of Mata Ortiz by a potter who noticed that when he signed his pots with a pencil, the signature remained metallic after the pot was fired. He began grinding pencil lead (graphite) into a powder and applying it to his pots. Quezada doesn't use this technique ("He thinks it's cheating," says Wisner), and no one in the village was willing to share their process with Wisner ("although you could see the graphite on everyone's hands"), so he experimented with various liquids to suspend the powdered graphite for application.

Water soaked into the pot too fast, leaving lumps of graphite on the surface.

Returning To The Roots

Once positioned, the oven-warmed pots are covered as quickly as possible with a metal bucket.

Wood stacked around the bucket is held in place with baling wire.

Sawdust (or dirt) is pushed around the base of the bucket to ensure an airtight seal.

Using lighter fluid on paper wads placed around the wood stack ensures an even burn.

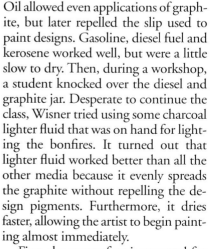

After 20–25 minutes of burning, the coals are raked away to allow cool-down.

Oil allowed even applications of graphite, but later repelled the slip used to paint designs. Gasoline, diesel fuel and kerosene worked well, but were a little slow to dry. Then, during a workshop, a student knocked over the diesel and graphite jar. Desperate to continue the class, Wisner tried using some charcoal lighter fluid that was on hand for lighting the bonfires. It turned out that lighter fluid worked better than all the other media because it evenly spreads the graphite without repelling the design pigments. Furthermore, it dries faster, allowing the artist to begin painting almost immediately.

First, the pot surface is prepared for burnishing (as described earlier). For a matt-pewter look, the sanding and/or baby-oil treatment is skipped. Working

Examining the results; sometimes, a propane torch is used to reoxidize (remove the carbon) from selected areas.

in a well-ventilated area, Wisner applies the graphite mixture with disposable 2½-inch sponge brushes, which allow even applications with no evidence of brushstrokes. The brush is dipped into the graphite mixture and wrung out until very little liquid remains. This prevents overapplication and running of the graphite slurry. The surface is allowed to dry until no wet spots remain (normally 1–2 minutes).

At this point, he gently rubs the entire piece with a clean, dry, cotton T-shirt to remove some of the graphite. This step reduces the graphite layer to the point where painted slip designs can adhere to the clay body underneath. Wisner originally applied a thick layer of graphite, taking a more-is-better approach, only to discover that the hours (or days) of design work would flake off easily after the firing.

After the excess graphite is rubbed off (a microfilm is all that is needed), he burnishes as described previously. For sculptural work or on vessels where there is to be no painted slip work, he doesn't worry about removing the excess. At this point, the thickly applied graphite can be burnished with fingers, forearm skin or a chamois. He always burnishes the most visible parts of a piece first to ensure they have the best shine. On large pieces, he applies graphite to sections as needed to allow enough "damp time" for effective burnishing.

To obtain traditional bonfiring results in a gas kiln, 1 to 2 inches of sawdust or horse manure are placed on a bed of sand.

A steel firing rack was constructed to maximize stacking space within a steel drum.

The drum is placed over the pottery and the sand is pushed against the bottom edge to ensure a good seal.

A Cone 012 firing takes about 30 minutes, followed by a 30-minute cool-down before removal.

Returning To The Roots

Hair Today, Brush Tomorrow

For painted designs, Wisner uses a thin slip made from Kentucky ball clay (OM 4) and, if painting on a white pot, mixes it with some black underglaze. The underglaze won't affect the final look, but the gray tone is easier to see on the slick surface. For fine lines, Wisner prefers a traditional Mata Ortiz brush made from human hair—a 1- to 3-inch piece of fine straight hair (15 to 20 strands is plenty) tied to the end of a stick (Wisner uses old bamboo chopsticks) with thread. Any "wild hairs" are removed to make a smooth brush that will pick up the clay paint without becoming too limp. Wisner says the women and children in Mata Ortiz are happy to provide a bit of their thick, straight hair. "You see them with locks missing all the time," he says.

Ready, Set, Fire

Firing is extremely low tech and may be accomplished in a backyard, a fireplace, a gas kiln or even a barbecue. For the black metallic surfaces, an intense reduction fire is necessary. The process requires a nongalvanized metal bucket (galvanization burns off, producing fumes during firing that, in addition to being toxic, leave a fog on the pottery surface), such as a paint bucket, coffee can or oil drum. It should be fired once to remove any paints or residues that might affect the clay.

The pots are preheated in an oven, kiln or in the sun for several hours. This drives out residual moisture in the clay body and greatly reduces firing mishaps. It is critical to keep the oven or kiln temperature below boiling. At the boiling point, water in the clay wall expands from a liquid to a gas (steam). The steam builds pressure rapidly and can easily pop out the pot wall.

Many fuels work in reduction fires. Thinly chopped firewood, cow dung and cottonwood tree bark all work well. Choose a site where the ground is dry. If this is not possible, a sheet of metal (not aluminum, which melts at 1000°F, or galvanized, for the reasons mentioned above) can serve as a vapor barrier. A 1- to 2-inch bed of sand serves

Handbuilt jars, to 18 inches in height, and slip-cast fish vessel, decorated with human-hair brushes.

as a base. This helps seal the metal bucket to create a reducing atmosphere. Well-dried dung (preferably range-fed animals) or sawdust from a pure wood source (not plywood or compressed board) is placed 1 to 3 inches deep on top of the sand.

It's best not to have the pottery touch the dung or sawdust because it sometimes causes blistering or undesirable flashing. (If flashing is desired, bisque fire the pot to Cone 018 in a kiln and fire it on top of or partially buried in the dung.) Baker's parchment paper is used to separate the pots from the dung. Another option is to stack the pots on kiln furniture or metal grates. The clay will not fully reduce where they touch. If the opening of one pot is covered by

another pot, Wisner puts a small handful of sawdust or dried dung in the lower pot to provide reduction for the upper pot's bottom.

The oven-heated pottery is transported to the firing site wrapped inside a cotton towel. Potters firing at a site far away from the oven can heat the pots (already thoroughly dried below the boiling point) to 300°F, wrap them in towels and place them in a cooler to keep them warm.

While a traditional bonfire is an easy, inexpensive method that yields excellent results, Wisner also achieves good results in a gas-fired kiln; not only is the firing easier to control, it is good for larger or thicker pieces (as well as in areas where bonfires might be illegal or inappropriate). This method was

"3 Amigos," 13 inches in height, slip-cast native clays, by Michael Wisner, Snowmass Village, Colorado.

developed in response to the cold Rocky Mountain winters at Anderson Ranch (at more than 8000 feet elevation). The radical cool-down after bonfirings sometimes caused cracking, so Wisner began experimenting with the same firing set-up within a gas kiln. Doug Casebeer, Anderson Ranch's clay program director, helped to refine the system using witness cones firing to Cone 014.

Wisner still uses sawdust or manure, a steel base, sand and the steel can to cover the work (as described above) but, instead of firewood, a gas kiln provides the external heat. He built a small gas kiln specifically for this process. It fires to Cone 012 in 30 minutes and cools within a half hour. Here, a cone pack with Cones 018, 014 and 012 helps determine the stopping points.

For a traditional bonfire, newspaper, charcoal lighter fluid and a few coat hangers or other flexible uncoated wire are useful in the next step. The metal can is placed over the oven-heated pots, and dirt or sawdust pushed up around the outside edge to create an airlock within the container. Firewood is stacked 5 to 8 inches thick around and as high as the bucket. The entire stack is wrapped with baling wire to ensure that the wood will stay erect during the fire. Three or four wads of paper are placed evenly

around the base of the wood, and doused with lighter fluid. The goal is to eliminate pottery breakage due to uneven heating.

The fire is lit and allowed to burn down completely. This will take 20–25 minutes. During this time, Wisner tends the fire with a long rake or stick, ensuring all the wood stays standing. A garden hose is kept nearby in case any peripheral vegetation catches fire.

The black coloration of a fired piece is achieved by virtue of carbon impregnation. As the firing chamber heats up, the internal fuel (dung or sawdust) ignites, liberating carbon. For a special effect, Wisner uses a small propane torch to selectively reoxidize (i.e., remove the black carbon) areas on a reduced piece. This is best done immediately after the firing, while the pots are still hot. This technique can have dramatic results when using a low-fire red talc body, leaving nice red areas next to the rich reduced black.

Reduction firing is where the graphite really shines. Graphite stays on the pottery surface to a much hotter temperature in reduction (to Cone 010) on most clay bodies. A safe window for this work is between Cone 018 and Cone 012. In that range, talc/ball clay bodies harden enough to have structural integrity and not dissolve in water. Additionally, within that range, the clay can maintain a burnish. Most lose their shine above Cone 010. Therefore, to satisfy both key firing criteria, shoot for a range between Cone 014 and 012.

The cool-down period lasts anywhere from 30 minutes to several hours, depending on the thickness of the pieces. To be conservative, pots may be cooled overnight and safely removed the following morning. Wisner works aggressively, cooling his pots only 30 minutes. This makes the firing about one hour from start to finish. Once the pots are cooled, they may be cleaned with a soft cotton cloth or washed with water. If all goes well, the fired pots will have an even black luster and the decorative designs, which will be matt black, will not flake or scratch off. ▲

Recipes

Mike's Mud
(Cone 012)

Texas Talc	50%
Kentucky Ball Clay (OM 4)	50
	100%
Add: Bentonite	2–5%

In a clean bucket, slake the ingredients in a large quantity of water, then stir vigorously. Let settle 10 to 15 seconds. Draw off the top 2 to 3 inches of liquid "cream."

Over a second bucket, strain the creamy layer through fabric, such as a T-shirt, or a 100-mesh screen to remove organic debris and small pieces of grog.

Add water to the original mixture in the first bucket and repeat until top water looks like skim milk after stirring and settling.

Let the strained clay (in the second bucket) sit for a few days—longer if clay is iron-bearing because the fine iron particles can stay suspended for several weeks. The mixture is ready to separate when the clay and water form two distinct layers. Decant the water. Stir the clay to rehomogenize. Pour/ladle it onto a plaster board or canvas sheet. Dry to a workable consistency. Store in clean plastic bags.

Painting Slip

For decorating slip (painting), mix 1 heaping teaspoon of Calgon water softener with 1 gallon water; add 2 pounds Kentucky ball clay (OM 4). Let settle for a few days. Draw off the water from the top and discard. Draw off the second "creamy" layer. Store in a jar; shake before use.

Note: Add a dash of commercial underglaze, such as Duncan Undercoat CC165. This colors the slip enough to see it when painting on burnished white clay but will not affect the color in the final fired body.

Graphite Slurry

To prepare graphite slurry, mix 2 tablespoons of fine graphite (available in tubes at most hardware stores) with 4 ounces lighter fluid (or substitute odorless lamp oil, diesel fuel or kerosene). Stir (or shake) it before use (in a well-ventilated area).

"Kings of Sea and Sky," 7½ inches in height, wheel thrown and coil built, burnished, brushed with terra sigillata, bisqued to Cone 018, smoked.

Freedom's Just Another Word

by Sumi von Dassow

Newsweek columnist George F. Will recently pooh-poohed the song lyrics "freedom's just another word for nothing left to lose." I can assure him from personal experience that Janice Joplin was right and he is wrong. A couple of summers ago, when my electric kiln refused to fire any longer to Cone 6, I gained the freedom to experiment with element-damaging combustion firing, and I haven't replaced those elements yet.

My last glaze firing took place on the hottest day of summer. I loaded my kiln and turned it on in the evening, hoping that before the morning climbed to un-

bearable heat the firing would have finished. The kiln had been taking longer and longer to reach temperature, but 14 hours should have been enough, so I turned it off by hand.

The problem was the kiln was in need of new elements, but I didn't have enough money to replace them just then. Besides, I'd always disliked glazing and longed to use my electric kiln to smoke-fire burnished pots.

Until then, concerns about damage to the elements had restrained me. At the time, I didn't belong to a co-op or know any potters with gas or raku kilns—and

all forms of open burning are banned in my county.

Taking advantage of the situation, I abandoned glazes and began coil building pots from red clay, burnishing the surfaces, applying terra sigillata, and firing them wrapped in newspaper in my electric kiln. These techniques are derived from the art of Pueblo potters of the Southwestern United States. Neither the wheel nor glazes are indigenous to America, and the best Native American pottery is still coil built and burnished.

Burnished pottery seems natural and yet exotic to one who is used to glazes.

The surface of a burnished pot is more tactilely inviting than cold, hard, slippery glazeware. A burnished surface is porous, thus warmer to the touch than a glazed one, while the clay's earthy hues enhance this impression of warmth.

A potter with a tendency toward perfectionism can rest assured that a glaze mishap is not going to ruin a burnished pot—no glazes will crawl or drip the wrong way, no bits of softbrick will embed themselves into a molten surface. This is liberating to one spending many hours lovingly forming and decorating a pot prior to consigning it to a kiln.

Once you've decided to burnish, the choice to coil build follows easily. The coil-built form with its slight asymmetries lends itself naturally to burnishing. Just as a hard coating of brightly colored glass seems appropriate on the machined roundness of a thrown pot, the imperfect curves and lines of a coiled pot demand to remain uncovered. By coil building, the potter is free to create any shape desired—a pot can have two necks, like the traditional Hopi wedding jar, or it can have an oval, square or triangular body.

Some Pueblo potters finish by firing their work entirely black, using the black-on-black effect of matt slip on the highly polished background achieved in a smothered combustion firing. An incompletely smothered fire only partially blackens a pot. Whenever smoke penetrates a burnished surface, the result is a pot ranging in color from deep velvety black to bright orange, an orange all the brighter in contrast to the black. This conjunction of coil building, burnishing and smoke firing allows the potter to achieve a disciplined yet unpredictable piece.

My work does not directly refer to Southwest tradition, despite borrowing elements of technique from Pueblo potters. It cannot be pigeonholed as Southwestern on the basis of burnishing and smoke firing. In fact, many of my forms seem closer in spirit to Hans Coper than to Maria Martinez, with decoration more reminiscent of the style of the Indians of the Pacific Northwest coast where I grew up. Other decorative styles that have influenced me are European folk pottery, Moslem tile work and early Mediterranean unglazed pottery.

When working, I don't consciously think about influences; the goal is to cre-

"Lords of Wind and Water," 8 inches in height, burnished earthenware with terra sigillata brushwork, smoke fired.

ate an object that cannot be experienced all at once, something that people can look at again and again and always see something new. I want people to appreciate the satiny smoothness of the burnished surface. I want them to look into the depths of the reflective surface, then pull back to see the pattern floating on top. I want the pattern to draw their eyes around the form. In sum, I want to create a pot that will, as much as a simple object can, interact with its viewers.

Experimenting with the kiln lent great freedom to my work. Responsibility to a

Rather than making a small pinchpot as a base for coil building, von Dassow prefers to throw a bottomless dome.

Once the top of the dome has been closed, the surface can be rounded and smoothed with a rib.

Returning To The Roots

"Four Horses," 12¼ inches in height, thrown and coiled earthenware, burnished, brushed with terra sigillata, smoked.

After the dome has become stiff enough to handle, it is turned upside down and placed in a *puki* (a footless bowl that spins freely on the work surface).

piece of equipment had hampered my creativity; I was struggling, without knowing it, simply to maintain an interest in clay. Freedom to misuse the kiln has rekindled the flame of enthusiasm. I've rediscovered creative joy and, as a bonus, my new work sells better than my old and fares better in juried competitions.

I use a smooth Cone 6 commercial clay. It might seem to make more sense to use a low-fire clay for burnished work, but low-fire clays tend to be soft and chalky and easily scratched if fired below their maturing temperatures. This particular clay is surprisingly sturdy even at Cone 018. Another reason not to use a low-fire clay is that nonclay materials added by the manufacturer to lower the maturing temperature tend to make these clays difficult to coil build. Coil building is a slow process; it makes all the difference having an easily workable clay.

I was taught to start a coil-built pot by making a small pinchpot as the base, then adding coils, but found this to be tedious and repetitive. An easier way is to throw a 6-inch-high bottomless dome to serve as the base of the pot. When the thrown dome section is stiff enough to handle, I turn it upside down and add coils to the top edge.

I work with the pot in a *puki*—the Indian word for a shallow bowl with no foot, only a rounded bottom, which spins freely on the work surface. It can function as a sort of extremely primitive wheel; while coil building, I can hold the coil in one hand and pinch with the other, without having to stop and turn the pot. When the pot is dry, I sand it smooth, then burnish with a stone.

Burnishing is a two-step process that can take two or three hours for a large pot, and once started must be finished without interruption. The first step is to moisten the whole pot lightly, then to re-wet small patches and rub with the stone until the clay becomes smooth and takes on a dull sheen. It is important to start at the rim, do the whole rim, then rub all the way around just below the rim, continuing in a spiral pattern from the rim toward the foot, because once a burnished patch has dried, it scratches if it is rubbed again with the stone. This is the reason that, once you begin, you can't stop until finished. Working in a spiral pattern ensures that you are never working on a

Because the puki turns freely, a coil can be held with one hand and joined with the other without stopping to turn the pot.

Wet burnishing is begun at the rim and spiraled downward to avoid scratching burnished patches that have dried.

patch adjacent to a section that has completely dried.

The second step is to immediately cover the entire pot with a light coating of vegetable oil. This soaks in and leaves a whitish scum on the surface. Rubbed again with the stone, the clay takes on a high gloss. I still marvel at the sight of plain clay polished so finely it reflects one's face like a mirror.

Once the pot is burnished, I sketch a design with a felt-tip pen—which doesn't scratch the delicate surface and the ink burns out at a low temperature—then paint with terra sigillata made from Cedar Heights Redart Clay (see Sandi Pierantozzi's recipe in the February 1993 CM). Since the burnished surface is very smooth (and somewhat greasy from the oil) and the terra sigillata tends to rub off easily, I mix in a small amount of CMC solution to make it stick. To make the solution, add 30 grams of CMC gum to a quart of boiling water, and continue to boil until it is dissolved. This solution is mixed by half teaspoons into the batch of terra sigillata until a brushed application can't be rubbed off with a finger. Too much CMC, and the terra sigillata can no longer be burnished easily just by rubbing with a

Terra sigillata is applied over a design sketched with a felt-tip pen.

chamois, so I have to be careful. I also am careful working with unfired burnished pottery, as it picks up fingerprints, and a drop of water or a stray drip of terra sigillata will damage the burnish.

Because it is the alignment of clay platelets that gives a burnished pot its sheen, and firing fuses these platelets, the

hotter a burnished pot is fired, the duller the surface becomes. Firing is thus a compromise between strength and beauty. I choose to bisque fire to Cone 018, at which point the clay sounds fired when tapped and is not easily scratched, but retains most of its sheen. The bisqued pot is then wrapped in one or two sheets of newspaper, then in a loose double layer of aluminum foil. After a brief firing, the result is a pot with a surface that varies from brick red to deep black, with the terra sigillata pattern varying in color from bright orange to silvery black.

Only then does the pot come to life. The firing in the "modified saggar," as I sometimes call my aluminum-foil wrapping, is like a bolt of lightning awakening the inert clay.

Of course, the use of an electric kiln for saggar firing voids its warranty and thus can't be recommended. I now use a gas kiln for this smoking step when possible. The use of a kiln, rather than the more traditional open fire, pit or sawdust-filled container, gives greater control over the final result and protection from cracking due to thermal shock. Saving one or two pots in this way could easily pay for new elements! ▲

Burnishing and Dung Firing

by Marsha Judd

With patience and good old-fashioned elbow grease, burnishing is a simple process that produces a brilliant sheen. Often I am asked, "What glaze is that?" I love to see the astonishment on people's faces when I reply, "There's no glaze; it's just the clay." Usually their astonishment quickly changes to curiosity about the process. And that's where I'll start.

Tool requirements are minimal. I have a collection of flat, rounded, smooth quartz stones that I keep in a bowl of water, along with a small silk sponge. I also use vegetable shortening. In fact, I still use the same container of Crisco I started burnishing with 10 years ago—a little goes a long way. A piece of used fine sandpaper and a lap-sized cloth (100% cotton) are the only other necessities—pretty basic stuff.

I work with a commercial, iron-rich, grog-free earthenware to which I have 5% pyrophyllite added. I have found that with this addition most red earthenwares will burnish brilliantly. I have also found that a commercial red sculpture body with 5% pyrophyllite can be burnished by using a flexible metal rib on the surface while the clay is still workable.

No slip or terra sigillata is applied. When the piece is bone dry, I start the burnishing process by lightly sanding the surface to remove salt scum that forms while drying. (I do not sand the sculpture clay.) Thoroughly dusted off, the piece is then "rough" burnished.

The purpose of this first burnishing step is to smooth the surface, mashing down any large grains of sand and bringing up the finer clay particles. Seated with the cloth on my lap, a burnishing stone in hand, and sponge and water at my side, I dab a little water on the surface and rub with my finger in a circular motion over a small area. I let the water just barely soak into the surface, then I begin rubbing with the stone, slowly but firmly, back and forth over the wet area. I repeat this step over the entire surface of the piece.

This rough burnish does not have to be perfect, but the surface should be smooth. You will see some lines, and it will not be shiny, just a dull sheen and a darker shade of red. The piece is now ready for polishing.

I start the polishing burnish in the same way as the rough burnish, checking my cloth for sand or loose clay and dust. After shaking it out, I start all over again, using Crisco this time instead of water, rubbing a minute amount into my palms, then rubbing the burnishing stone between my palms. (Don't put Crisco directly onto the work.)

"Caught Between the Things We Cannot Control," 25 inches in length, burnished, dung-fired earthenware, by Marsha Judd, Fullerton, California.

With a little bit of Crisco and a whole lot of elbow grease, the surface immediately begins to shine. I put more Crisco on my palm as needed (when the stone is binding up on the surface or when I feel my palms drying out). Using the backside edge of my stone, I work patiently, frequently examining the surface for imperfections, adjusting the pressure as required. The proof is always in the surface. If it's shining, you've got it.

After burnishing, the piece is bisque fired slowly to Cone 022. Bisquing to this temperature allows a fair degree of maturity in earthenware bodies, without compromising the burnishing.

The structural stability achieved in the bisque prepares the piece for a dung fire, which creates blacks, silvers, oranges, browns and reds. Firing with dung is not always predictable, but years of practice have given me some worthwhile tips to share.

I think of my original firings in a washtub full of holes, and I wonder what my neighbors must have thought. I now fire inside a 22-cubic-foot softbrick kiln. I have also used hardbrick and fiber kilns. But if you intend to do this in your kiln, remember there will be ash after firing that should be thoroughly removed.

I start by building a brick saggar inside the kiln, then fill it with a 1-inch-thick layer of ash, topped by 1 to 2 inches of shredded manure. (I buy manure at a home-improvement store.) I then carefully stack my pieces in the saggar, filling in with manure as needed. Finally, the saggar is covered with kiln shelves (2-inch-thick fiber blanket can also be used). I load very methodically; openings in the bricks of the saggar or proximity to the top of the saggar are crucial in determining where and which colors will be achieved.

To achieve those colors and smoke effects, I fire subjectively, by sight and smell; wet or damp manure burns more

"One on Top of the Other," 14 inches in height, thrown, paddled, burnished and chipped earthenware.

slowly and differently than dry. Cones are irrelevant to what's actually going on inside your saggar.

When I want reds and oranges, I fire until I can no longer smell a pungent odor in the air. The interior of the kiln will be bright orange. Once both of these occur, I turn off the gas, and leave both port holes and dampers open. Complete cooling takes about 24 hours.

For blacks, the interior of the kiln will be red, and the air will be slightly pungent. That's when I turn off the gas and shut the damper and ports completely. The pungent smell will continue for at least 6–8 hours, and the saggar will take approximately 48 hours to cool completely.

Silver is the toughest and the most unpredictable surface to achieve, but oh so exciting when you unearth it. My secret is damp manure. Actually, I mist it as I'm loading the saggar, layering damp and dry, damp and dry. This allows a little more placement control, but (there's always a "but") the silver's permanency is achieved only by total suffocation at the firing's end. Again, there will be a pungent smell, and the saggar will take 48 hours to cool.

I made my first attempts at burnishing and dung firing in 1981. Thirteen years later I can say I think I've got it; determination knows no bounds. But as determined as I was to perfect surfaces, they are only in humble homage to all those who worked in this way

"The Ups and Downs of It," 18 inches in length, burnished earthenware with chipped surfaces, fired in a manure-filled saggar.

Returning To The Roots

before me. Whether these potters burnished for function or for surface effect, the common thread that ties us all together was and is our dedication to clay as our way of life. And in that dedication resides an intimacy between artist and clay, knowing your material,

Most of Judd's rock forms start off as wheel-thrown "balloons"; however, large forms are sometimes coil built.

acknowledging what you do and do not have control over, reveling in its beauty, and respecting its limitations. For me, the process and results of burnishing are a metaphor for life itself: beautifully fragile, stoic yet unforgiving, mysterious and forever enduring. ▲

The bone-dry piece is "rough" burnished by dabbing water on the surface and rubbing with a stone.

After the rough burnish, the surface will be smooth, but not shiny—just a dull sheen.

A highly reflective sheen is accomplished by polishing with a Crisco-rubbed stone.

The saggar is built inside a 22-cubic-foot gas kiln; firing duration depends on the results desired.

After a Cone 022 bisque firing, the burnished forms are stacked with manure inside a brick saggar.

When filled, the saggar is covered with kiln shelves; 2-inch-thick fiber blanket may also be used.

After cooling for 48 hours, burnished, dung-fired pieces need nothing more than a quick dusting off.

Magdalene Odundo

Born in Nairobi, raised in India, then schooled in art in Kenya and England, Magdalene Odundo draws inspiration for her handbuilt terra-cotta vessels from diverse cultures. However, she remains "firmly rooted in the vessel-making tradition," says David Queensberry, a partner of Queensberry Hunt Design Consultants and formerly Odundo's teacher at the Royal College of Art. "It is important to her that her pots are containers; in this respect they seem to have a function, but they cannot be said to be utilitarian... Her work, like that of many contemporary studio ceramists, must be seen as an aesthetic quest.

"There is a paradox for a potter like Magdalene—making containers destined to remain empty when the references are mainly ceramics from the past, which were utilitarian. Nearly all pottery, though, shows signs of being made with two purposes in mind: utility and aesthetic pleasure. Indeed, it is quite difficult to find examples of pottery where some part of the work has *not* been carried out to achieve characteristics that are unrelated to utility. Attaining an abstract excellence in artifacts seems deeply rooted in the human psyche. One could argue that this is the origin of art.

"The qualities in Magdalene's work are conditioned by the way she makes her pots, and the materials and processes that she uses, particularly the way her work is fired."

Odundo's pots are coil built, then scraped smooth, slip coated and burnished. Color depends on the firing atmosphere. Her orange/rust pots are once fired in oxidation in a gas-fueled fiber kiln; the blackware is the result of a second firing—each piece packed with combustibles in a saggar (made for her by Wedgwood) for reduction.

"Magdalene exploits the possibilities inherent in this way of working—with skill and sensitivity," Queensberry concludes. "Her pots prove that it is quite possible to make statements in clay with forms that, while not being overtly sculptural, have the same purity that one finds in the work of sculptors like Brancusi. It is not necessary for a potter to cut the umbilical cord with the vessel to make work that can be taken seriously as sculpture." ▲

Magdalene Odundo (Bentley, Hants, England) with simple tools for making burnished ware in her studio.

"Angled Mixed-Color Piece," 15 inches in height, coil-built terra cotta, burnished, reduction fired with combustibles in a saggar.

"Mixed-Color Reduced Symmetrical Piece," 14 inches in height,
coil-built terra cotta, smoked with combustibles inside a saggar.

"Symmetrical Narrow-Necked Tall Piece," approximately 17 inches in height, coil-built, burnished and reduced terra cotta, by Magdalene Odundo.

Obviously, it is possible to pit or saggar fire either wheel-thrown or handbuilt work. However, some pottery forms may work better than others. Most potters who use these firing methods prefer to stick with fairly simple, round pots. There are two reasons for this. The first reason is that the complexity of surface created in a pit-type firing calls for a simple form. The second reason is that something wide and shallow, such as a platter, or a form with projecting parts or added elements, might be more vulnerable to cracking due to heat stress. For this reason, it's also best to fire pieces with relatively thin, even walls. A wheel-thrown pot can easily meet these requirements, by being created from a single piece of clay and trimmed to a uniform thickness.

In coil building for pit firing, it is important to work the coils together thoroughly and avoid letting the pot dry too much between coils. Any abrupt change of contour may be particularly vulnerable, as coils may be weakly joined together at such a point. In addition, such a form may channel heat and flame unevenly, leading to heat stress. This is not to imply that coil-built work is unsuitable for pit firing. The more organic character of a coil-built form is appropriate to these types of firing, this marriage of low-tech forming and firing methods creating an aesthetic unity. After all, both techniques precede the inventions of the wheel and the kiln, and traditional Native American and African pottery is still coil built and fired in the open.

Slab-built work may be more difficult to fire successfully due to a certain inherent weakness at the joints. If two pieces of slab are joined to form a corner, the joining should be done while the clay is fairly wet and the clay worked together well. If slabs are joined by overlapping the ends, the form will be thicker at the join, which should be minimized if possible. Experimentation with various forms, clay bodies, and firing methods has led many potters to success. A complex form may fare better fired singly in a barrel filled with sawdust, or in a saggar, than with other pots in an open pit.

Though pit firing and related techniques do not yield fully functional ware, that is clearly a liberating factor, allowing potters to take individual paths to an inspiring diversity of approach.

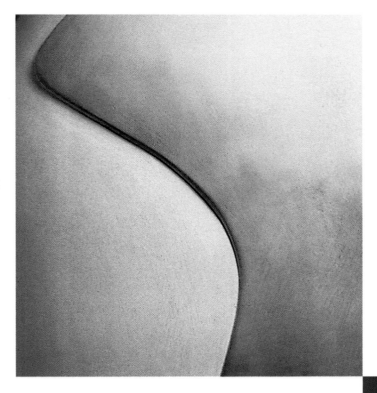

Collaboratively thrown vessels, to approximately 16 inches in height, burnished and sawdust fired.

Collaborative Throwing

by Susan and Jim Whalen

Collaboration among potters is not a new idea. There's something about clay and the process of working with it that entices people to work together. Besides the practical aspect of "many hands making light work," the receptive nature of clay itself influences those who work with it, making it easier to break down boundaries and share individual concepts. By using collaboration as an area of in-depth exploration, not just a tool, we have made many discoveries about ourselves and about clay. As we became more receptive to one another in our exploration, we became more claylike in nature. This led to deeper appreciation and understanding of the material, and generated a powerful creative process that continues to provide the energy and ideas to take us further into what we are doing.

The physical mechanism that sets the whole thing in motion is throwing together on the wheel. Working on the wheel is basically a personal and intimate experience. To share that experience requires an open and relaxed state of mind, plus constant communication. We started doing it just for fun. Despite how meaningful the technique has become, the fun element is alive and well.

We began by making a bowl together. That was so much fun, we made a few more. We then started throwing larger and larger masses of clay, producing some planters and simple jars. Next, we went back to making bowls, producing a series of large, footed bowls, which were glazed and fired to Cone 7.

After the bowls, we started throwing large, round, closed forms. Susan had burnished and pit fired one of our ear-

lier pots. We liked the look so much we wanted to see it in larger scale. This meshed with our desire to see how big a piece of seamless pottery we could make with four hands. As a result, the pieces are becoming planetary in appearance, the markings from the pit firing suggesting drifting continents, weather masses, night and day.

Our technique keeps evolving as we apply what we learn from each piece to the next. No, it's not like that scene in *Ghost.* Susan sits in the traditional position and runs the foot pedal. Jim sits directly across on a chair or sometimes on the wheel table. Two pieces of wedged clay are joined on the wheel and patted down, forming a mound that is round and as centered as possible. We then push the clay up into a cone by using pressure from all four hands. The cone

Four hands are better than two when centering a large mass of clay on the potter's wheel.

An opening is made by wedging all four hands together and pushing down into the center.

The first few pulls are made by pressing in with the heels of the outside hands.

Finger pulls are made, usually in the same groove, until the pot is in danger of collapse.

If the shape starts to expand too much, all four hands are used to collar it back in.

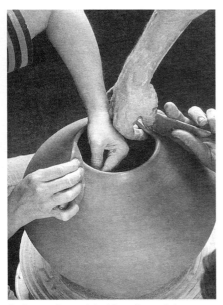
Collapse is avoided by alternately expanding the shape with ribs and drying it with a heat gun.

Once the potters agree the shaping is done, the rim is smoothed; then the pot is removed from the wheel and dried under plastic for several days.

Trimming with two sets of hands goes quite fast and keeps the pot more symmetrical.

Sawdust-fired vessel, 15 inches in diameter, collaboratively thrown, trimmed and burnished, by Susan and Jim Whalen, Charlotte, North Carolina.

is brought back down by using two points of pressure, Susan's hands on top of Jim's. An opening is made by wedging our hands together and pushing down into the center. We then form the bottom by pulling straight back from each other.

The first one or two pulls are made with the heels of our outside hands to get the thick mass of clay moving. This brings a lot of clay up and keeps it contained at the same time. We trim a little clay away from the bottom so we can get under the wall to start raising it with our fingers. With a "ready-set-go," we start pulling the clay up and out to form the rounded cylinder.

A lot of attention is paid to the inside shape. If it's starting to expand too much, we use all four hands to collar it back in. We have brought large expanding pieces back in with four hands that would have been impossible for two.

We keep bringing the clay up, usually throwing in the same groove until it's in danger of collapse. At this point, we either leave it alone to stiffen or fan it with a heat gun. We may then try another pull or begin expanding it with wooden ribs.

We alternate expanding the shape with ribs and drying it with the heat gun until we get the upper two thirds of the pot the way we want it. The large dome top can be tricky. Four hands have come to the rescue more than once, holding up a collapsing wall and frantically drying it with the heat gun. Once we agree that shaping is done, we finish the rim and let the pot dry evenly under plastic for several days.

When hard enough to trim, the pot is inverted and often placed in a chuck (a weighted 5-gallon bucket) on the wheel head. Trimming together goes quite fast and keeps the pot more symmetrical. We then dampen and smooth the surface in preparation for burnishing with large spoons. Larger pots are burnished on the wheel.

Once the pot is dry, it is bisque fired to Cone 016, then sawdust fired in a perforated 55-gallon drum. We use dry hardwood shavings/sawdust as the primary combustible and add small amounts of natural materials for random effects. Charcoal lighter is used to ignite the combustibles; we mix it with some of the sawdust, then pour it on top of the pottery and sawdust, and

light it. We try for fast, hot firings that are as smokeless as possible to keep the pots from turning all black, and to avoid problems with the city fire department.

The clay is an unrefined yellow clay from Bethune, South Carolina. We get it pretty much the way it comes out of the ground. This is not a clay body; it's a clay. It's inconsistent, varies from batch to batch, and contains rocks, sand, mica and organic matter. It sometimes causes cracks, craters and asymmetry in our pots, but it throws and burnishes well. The amazing range of subtle coloration it provides and additional surface interest from its impurities make it perfect for sawdust firing.

Unless you're jaded or totally practical, working on the wheel with another person is magic. Each touch may be a split second apart and modifying as it goes, but the alternation blends into one touch in our minds. The effects of this energy exchange have enhanced what we're doing individually in clay as well. You may want to try collaborative throwing as a way of making big pottery or for exploring the creative duality of life. Whatever the reason, we're sure you'll have fun. ▲

A Sense of Timelessness

by Jimmy Clark

"Globe Pot," 14 inches in height, pinched, brushed with terra sigillata, pit fired, partially stripped, sanded and sealed, by Jimmy Clark, Philadelphia.

Pinching is an ancient handbuilding technique that allows the maker to interact directly with the clay. In my work, the consistency of the material, its reactions to atmospheric conditions and my own mood or subconscious are given free rein to affect the final form. The desired result is a sense of timelessness—a sense that the pot has had a long life of its own, independent of its creator. Ultimately, I like to think of myself as but one of three integral elements that share equal responsibility for the work's creation: artist, material, and fire.

My vessels are freely formed while resting on my lap or in sling molds made by loosely spanning a bucket or other round container with a towel. I do have several start-up techniques that direct the pot toward a particular shape (i.e., oval, tall, open or closed), but often I find the clay leading in a totally different direction, and have learned that following the clay is vastly preferable to struggling with it.

Despite a preoccupation with larger forms in recent years, I usually restrict myself to pinching the piece out of a single ball of clay. At one time, I explored the size limitations of this process and pinched out an entire 25-pound bag of prepared clay, but for the most part my larger forms begin as 10- to 15-pound balls.

I like to think of these pots as asymmetrical balloons blown up to the brink of bursting. The walls of the resulting forms are often extremely thin and fragile. Sometimes, this fragility leads to breakage of one kind or another, but in recent years I have begun to incorporate these occurrences as yet another event contributing to the vessel's history and ultimate appearance.

The most common forms of breakage are what I refer to as "spirit holes," inspired by the spirit bowls of the ancient Mimbres of the Southwest. I have come to appreciate these small breakthroughs, which often occur during burnishing, and their seemingly predestined

"Storage Jar with Spirit Hole," 12½ inches in height, pinched from a single ball of clay, brushed with terra sigillata, and pit fired in sawdust.

"Bowl," 12 inches in height, pinched, brushed with terra sigillata, pit fired, partially stripped, sanded and sealed, then accented with inlaid copper.

placement as enhancements to the form. Other more dramatic mishaps, which may occur during firing or through random accidents, may be addressed by inserting copper patches and decorating with metallic paint.

Concluding this intuitive approach is my preferred firing method—pit firing—which blackens the surfaces in totally unpredictable and uncontrollable ways. To achieve deep blacks, I used to purposely retard the firings, allowing very little air into the kiln and burning the finest sawdust I could find. One particularly slow-burning firing retained glimmering ashes eleven days after ignition. More recently, however, I have become fasci-

"Bottomless Pot with Brass Stand," 10½ inches in height, pinched, rubbed with crocus martis, burnished and pit fired, by Jimmy Clark.

nated with the flashings and color variations that come with faster firings done with coarser sawdust and increased air flow.

The larger scale of my recent work has led me to experimenting with terra sigillata. Applications to bisqueware resulted in a glorious "mistake," where most of the sigillata peeled off like bad paint in the pit fire. After the balance was scraped off, a singularly rich and varied pattern (resembling spider webs intertwined with cartography) remained.

In addition to the peeled-terra-sigillata technique, I have begun to subject the pots to mutiple firings. I find that these more varied surfaces increase the sense of "history" for each vessel. ▲

"Bowl with Copper Patch," 9½ inches in height, pinched, brushed with terra sigillata, broken, pit fired and reassembled.

A Soulful Sound

by Janie Rezner

Janie Rezner playing a triple ocarina.

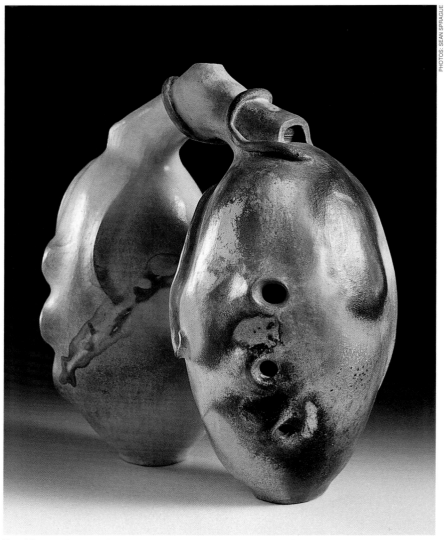

Double ocarina, 7¼ inches in height, handbuilt, saggar fired and waxed.

I have sung all my life, having been blessed with a musical mother with a beautiful voice, who hummed and sang around the house as she worked and as she played the piano. Singing came as naturally to me as breathing. My mother was born in 1893 in the little town of Oquawka, Illinois, where her mother and grandmother had lived their entire lives. I grew up on the outskirts of Biggsville (population 200), just 12 miles from Oquawka, where my father farmed the same 160 acres that his father and grandfather had farmed.

Everything was small back then; there were 19 in my high-school class, 80 students in the whole school. I sang in a trio in high school. My mother was our arranger. We sang for meetings, weddings, funerals, our own graduation and for Adlai Stevenson when he came through town; we sang on local radio and on the Morris B. Sack's Amateur Hour (won $75 and a gold watch).

I went on to Monmouth College, majored in music, married and raised three children in Iowa, singing all the while. I moved to California in 1979, and went on to earn a master's degree in clinical psychology. It wasn't until about five years ago, however, that I first heard the ocarina, played before a reading at a bookstore in Berkeley. I was enthralled by this mystical-sounding instrument that plays three tones at once. With my background in harmonizing, it had a special appeal to me. Through the performer, I contacted the instrument's cre-

ator, Sharon Rowell, and spent the next four months learning how to make ocarinas from her. For the past three years, I have made them as an artist-in-residence at the Mendocino Art Center.

The triple ocarina is finely tuned. The front two chambers play a full scale, while the back chamber plays two notes and is played with the heel of the hand. Thus, one can play three-part harmony.

The chambers come together at the top into a single divided mouthpiece, divided so that the front two chambers can be played without the back cham-

ber. I make double-chambered ocarinas as well. They, too, are soulful sounding, their two voices weaving in and out.

Using high-fire sculpture mix, I create a chamber by putting two pinchpots together as an egg shape. Placement of the fingerholes does not seem to have a bearing on the tone, and is determined by where my fingers rest while holding the instrument. The larger the chambers, the deeper the tone. My ocarinas range in size from 6 to 9 inches in height and 7 to 8 inches across.

While the clay is still moist, I make

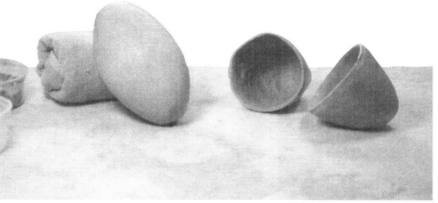

Two pinch pots form a sound chamber; double- and triple-chambered ocarinas are joined at the top with a single mouthpiece.

an aperture on one end of the egg; the aperture has a sharp slant, or blade, on one side. A small piece of clay with a thin opening (windway) is fastened above the aperture so that air being blown through it will hit the blade. This creates the sound. I tune as I work; however, I can't blow too much on wet clay; otherwise, the windway will collapse. Once the form is completed, I burnish the surface to a smooth finish.

After a bisque firing, the ocarinas are either fired in a pit (a large Weber barbecue works well) or a saggar in an outdoor raku kiln. I put in copper carbonate, salt, a little wood and sometimes a few long grasses wrapped around the ocarinas for patterning, and start the fire. I never know what I'll get, but I generally love the results. Sometimes they come out in pink fleshy tones with shiny black areas here and there. Recently, I've been getting rich browns and tans with touches of orange and red.

Afterward, they are scrubbed and tuned for the final time, then waxed and polished. The final tuning is subtle, and having a good "ear" is essential. Slight alterations can be made by either filing on the inside of a fingerhole, to lower the tone, or by putting a little epoxy on the inside, to raise the tone. I prefer to tune the unison notes slightly off from each other, creating a wonderful vibration between the notes. ▲

Triple ocarina, 7 inches in height, by Janie Rezner, Mendocino, California.

Handbuilt Vessels

by Dale Allison Hartley

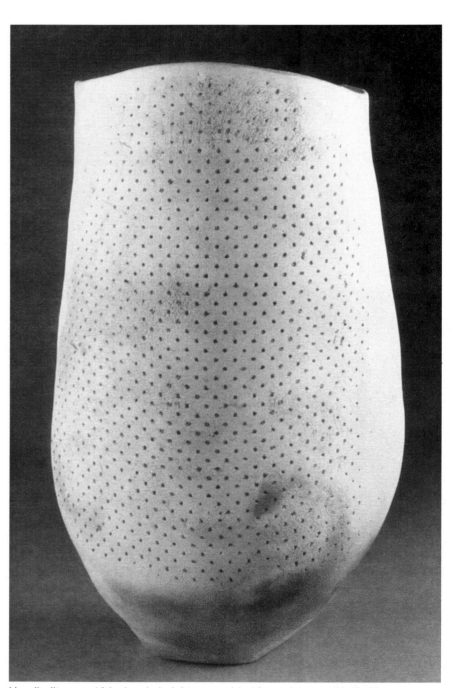

Handbuilt vase, 16 inches in height, assembled from slump-molded white stoneware slabs, low salt fired, by Dale Allison Hartley, Emporia, Kansas.

Living in the Flint Hills of Kansas, I am inspired by the subtle rolling landscape, soft clear light, spaciousness and simplicity. Over time, my slab-built vessels have become simpler, yet they continue to reveal a similar graceful motion. The surfaces are lightly textured with sand or roadside gravel that I enjoy collecting wherever we travel.

For many years I worked mainly with a white stoneware clay body, enjoying the simplicity and concentrating on the forms. Now, when rolling the slabs with a large rolling pin, I use silica sand and grog as ball bearings for the clay to spread out on, in addition to texturing the surface.

I began working with clay when I was very young. My mother is an artist, and she encouraged creative activities. In high school, I found my way to the ceramics room whenever I could. It followed then that in college I would focus on clay and art education, subsequently earning an M.A. in ceramics at Emporia State University.

When my husband and I moved to a small rural community in Kansas, the Tallgrass Prairie was like a different world to us. I set up my studio in a two-car-garage-sized building adjacent to our house, then built tables out of packing crates and installed two used kilns. There was a lot to do. When I took breaks, I often walked to the local grain elevator, which gave me the opportunity to observe the natural world around me.

For my claywork, I was seeking a light and free feeling. As I explored the possibilities, several methods of construction developed. One involves draping clay slabs over cardboard cutout slings and assembling the slump-molded sections. This cardboard cutout method began when I was looking for a bowl to drape some clay into. I decided to cut out a circle in some cardboard instead. This led to assembling two halves and

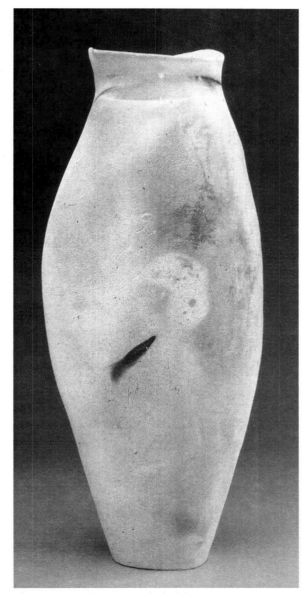

"Ontario Vase," 27 inches in height, slump-molded stoneware.

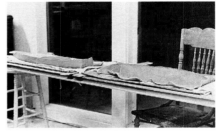

Two clay slabs are placed in fabric-draped, cardboard-cutout slings and allowed to stiffen, then joined together with a coil at the seam.

standing them on end. Sometimes three sections are joined together.

I begin by drawing a shape on cardboard, then cut out the hole. The edges of these cardboard cutouts are placed on 2×4 supports and a piece of fabric material is lightly draped over the hole to support the clay. Once the material has sagged to the depth I want for shaping the clay slab, it is secured with staples or tape. Two clay slabs are placed in cutout slings and allowed to stiffen. Sometimes clay walls are added to the edges of these halves to increase the width of the piece.

Thin dry-cleaner plastic helps control drying. I cut strips and place them on the edges that need to remain moist for attachment. When the sections are stiff enough to keep from collapsing, I put one half on top of the other half and add a coil at the seam. The piece is then allowed to firm up before it is stood upright.

The next stage is the most exciting. It's at this point that I decide what the form is actually going to evolve into. Sometimes it is as if the final shape is already there and I am just discovering it. I tend to encourage asymmetrical balance and graceful lines, trying to create within each piece a presence that is soft, subtle and light, yet portrays poise and strength.

Some areas are allowed to be rough and free; others are refined, but I try to preserve the freshness of the surface by not overworking the clay. Smoothing the seams can take a tremendous amount of time.

I use a variety of firing processes. Presently, it is fun to collaborate with the fire, allowing flashing from the sodium vapors of low-fire salting to gently color the surfaces. If this results in undesirable effects, I sometimes spray over areas with colored slips. This requires another firing, but allows me to continue working on a piece until I am satisfied. Also, enamels used by metalsmiths are sometimes added for color and a saltlike effect. ▲

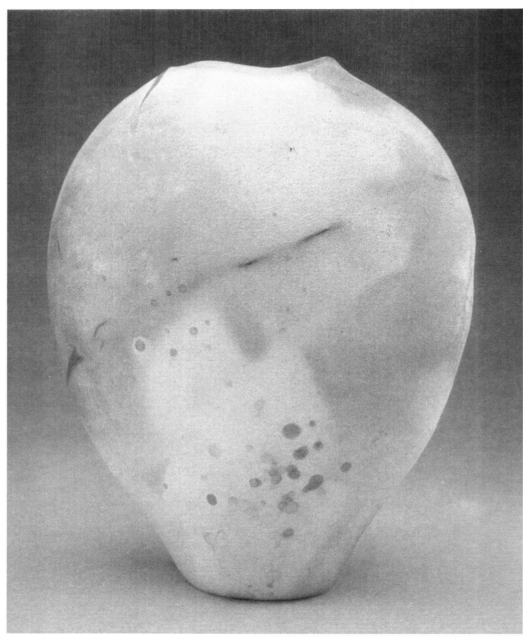

"Sausolito Vase," 19 inches in height, slab-built stoneware, low salt fired.

Hartley's studio is in a two-car-garage-sized building adjacent to her house.

Clay, Nails and Smoke

by Jerry Caplan

Combining nonceramic materials with clay has long been of interest to me. It all started with the use of copper tacks. The original idea was to affect the color of glaze by leaching copper oxide out of tacks pressed into the clay surface. Those copper tacks served their purpose, but they also led to experiments with steel nails, as these could withstand higher temperatures and could be used for structural purposes as well as decoratively. Ordinary household nails were soon followed by rods, bolts, metal stampings and finally, (expensive) stainless steel turkey skewers.

Nails of a very special kind emerged as the most effective. These are called gimp tacks or linoleum nails. They measure about ⅝ to ¾ inches in length, and have a stout shank and rounded head. While these are small, they do a fine job of joining slabs of clay securely, but avoid cracking problems during drying. Even heavier nails work well if they are given a little wiggle as they enter the clay. The thicker the nail, the greater the wiggle required to allow for some shrinkage of the clay on the unshrinking nail.

Using nails as a fastener instead of slip results in a much more spontaneous joint and allows one to literally "draw in the air." Interestingly, nailing clay is not unlike nailing wood except that clay has tremendous plasticity and can be bent or warped. I use a white stoneware and add about 10% medium grog if the work is to be smoke surfaced.

None of the recent forms have bottoms, partly for philosophical reasons and partly for practical reasons. The series of teapots, which were made over foam-rubber shapes, have a rectangular opening through which the foam rubber can be retrieved when the piece has stiffened sufficiently to hold its shape. Other works are bottomless to place emphasis on sculptural form rather than function. The teapot metaphor contains all the parts—body, spout, handle and lid—but these are all perceived as active components of a sculptural statement.

After bisque firing, glaze is applied to selected areas of the nailed piece, which is then returned to the kiln for a Cone 05 firing. Thereafter, lusters are added and the piece refired to Cone 018. Lastly, the work is smoked briefly in burning newspapers, aided by a stream of air from a reversed vacuum cleaner hose (blowing out instead of drawing in).

A cairn of bricks built around the piece with space to allow for crumpled newspaper between the brick and the work becomes a kind of loose kiln. As courses rise around the pot, newspapers are added at each level. Finally, the top is partly closed with bricks or covered with a piece of tin. The paper is ignited through spaces left between the bricks. The stream of air from the vacuum cleaner is fed in through these same openings at the bottom, raising the temperature considerably. While this creates a good deal of smoke, the firing is very short in duration, approximately five to ten minutes. Interesting localized reduction/carbonization can be achieved and controlled to some extent by careful arrangement of the crumpled newspaper when stacking and charging the cairn.

The result is a dialogue between the ruggedness of nails, the elegance of lusters and the intrigue of unglazed surfaces where the smoke is allowed to do its dirty work. ▲

"Aggressive Teapot Form," 10 inches in height, stoneware with nails, lusters and metal knob, smoked in newspapers.

"Blue Teapot Form," 10 inches in height, slab built from white stoneware using nails as fasteners, surfaced with lusters.

Jerry Caplan constructing a stoneware and nail teapot around
a foam-rubber form in his Pittsburgh studio.

To hasten stiffening of a damp clay slab, heat from a propane
torch is applied where needed.

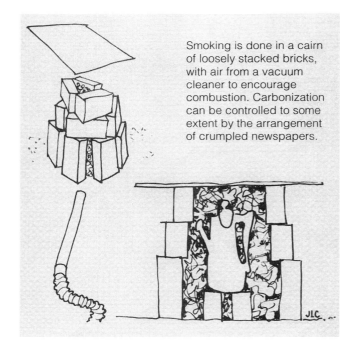

Smoking is done in a cairn
of loosely stacked bricks,
with air from a vacuum
cleaner to encourage
combustion. Carbonization
can be controlled to some
extent by the arrangement
of crumpled newspapers.

A Female Form

The Sculpture Techniques of Margaret Keelan

by Benny Shaboy

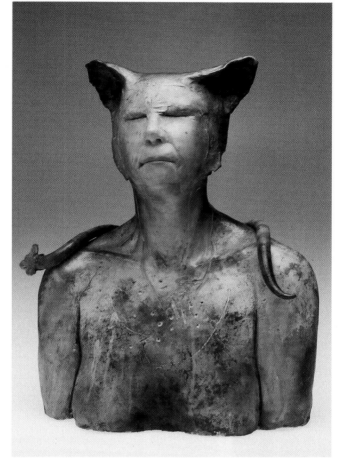

"Me and My Cat," 20 inches in height, press molded and handbuilt, with polished terra sigillata, smoked.

Margaret Keelan refers to her ceramic sculptures as "comments on interior landscape, alternative personalities, memories and tribal influences." She bases them on the female form, she says, "to keep them as close to my own self-image as I can."

The Canadian-born sculptor is currently an assistant director of sculpture at the San Francisco Academy of Art College. Although she has explored several different ceramic techniques during the last 26 years, she has become especially interested in low-fire surface finishes during the years she has been teaching at the academy. Recently, she has been combining terra-sigillata accents with raku effects. Her palette of raku glazes is purposely limited to a dry patina and a clear crackle, along with some oxide embellishments.

Each piece is one of a kind, but she sometimes makes a press mold of a form so that she can produce variations. What comes out of the mold serves mainly as a base. She will often cut a piece into sections before the firing, planning to glue it back together afterward. This allows her to raku the sections individually, sometimes giving each section a different treatment.

Although her methods vary from piece to piece, the following paragraphs detail the production of "Woman with Turban 1":

First, Keelan formed a female torso about 25 inches in height, keeping the features simple and the surfaces smooth. From that, she made a two-part plaster mold. When the plaster was dry, she rolled out slabs of a mid-range stoneware, and pressed them into the mold.

The resulting figure was similar to the original, except that she sliced off the bottom 5 inches. Next, she cut it into sections: the dress, top of the dress to near the eyes, a "mask" area around the eyes, and the turban. She then applied an underglaze to the eyes, and brushed a terra sigillata on the turban, buffing it with a flannel cloth when dry.

During a bisque firing to Cone 04, the dress was broken, but that is "the kind of happy accident" she welcomes, "because you simply raku each piece separately and take advantage of the differences in finish."

She accented the lips and the edge of the dress with oxides, then applied a clear raku crackle glaze to the dress sections (leaving the natural color of the clay to show through). The rest of the coloring on the finished sculpture is carbon from the post-firing reduction.

Because she lives in a fairly urban section of the San Francisco Bay Area, she has to move quickly to avoid releasing too much smoke into the air. "You want to make it look like you're barbecuing or constantly trying to start a barbecue," Keelan jokes.

As a last step, she used a black epoxy to glue all the pieces together and to fill

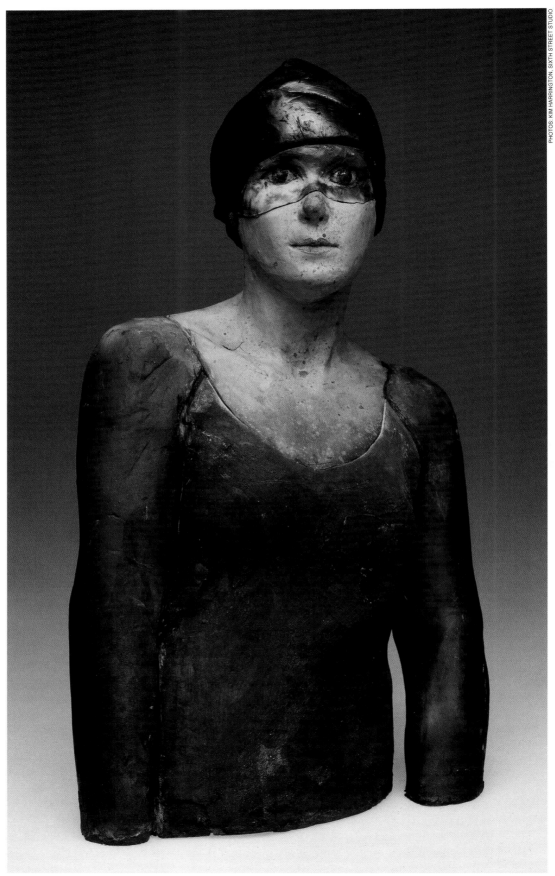

"Woman with Turban 3," 25 inches in height, press molded and handbuilt, with terra sigillata, raku fired.

any gaps, cleaning off the excess with rubbing alcohol.

Before she started working with raku, she often designed pieces, such as "Me and My Cat," explicitly for a terra-sigillata finish. To make terra sigillata, she fills about one-fourth of a quart jar with clay, adds one teaspoonful of deflocculant (Darvan or sodium silicate), fills the rest of the jar with water, then shakes vigorously. After the solution has settled for about a week, she uses a turkey baster to draw off excess water at the top, then simply dips her brush into the fine particles remaining in suspension at the top. After the applied terra sigil-

lata has dried on the clay, she polishes it with a flannel cloth.

On the cat piece, she applied several layers of terra sigillata, some of which had been mixed with commercial stains for color variety. Since the latter are coarser than the former, she would sometimes apply a layer of plain terra sigillata over the stained variation to allow the color to come through, yet still develop a good shine.

Once the terra-sigillata pieces have been fired to Cone 010 in an electric kiln, extra depth and richness are sometimes added by a technique Keelan calls "smoking"—a process that

involves holding a sheet of newspaper against the piece with raku tongs, then liberally dousing everything with charcoal briquette starter, and lighting. The carbon from the burning newspaper adds a patina to the clay body that ranges from light gray all the way to black.

Keelan enjoys exploring the different surface treatments. Although it takes a long time to master a technique, the effort is worthwhile, she says, because of the richness of the results. She also likes to experiment "because it's a way to identify oneself, a way to see one's self grow." ▲

To smoke the interior of this head, charcoal barbecue starter was poured onto newspaper and lit; the burning newspaper was then held against the inner wall of the piece with raku tongs.

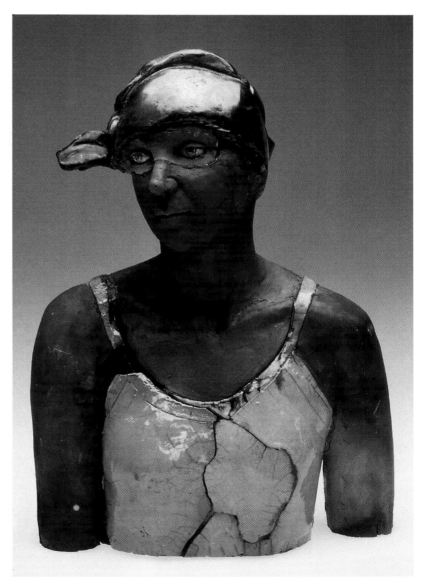

"Woman with Turban 1," 20 inches in height, press molded and handbuilt, with terra sigillata (turban) and crackle glaze (dress), raku fired, by Margaret Keelan, San Pablo, California.

Forming Techniques for Pit and Saggar Firing

Jean-Luc Mas

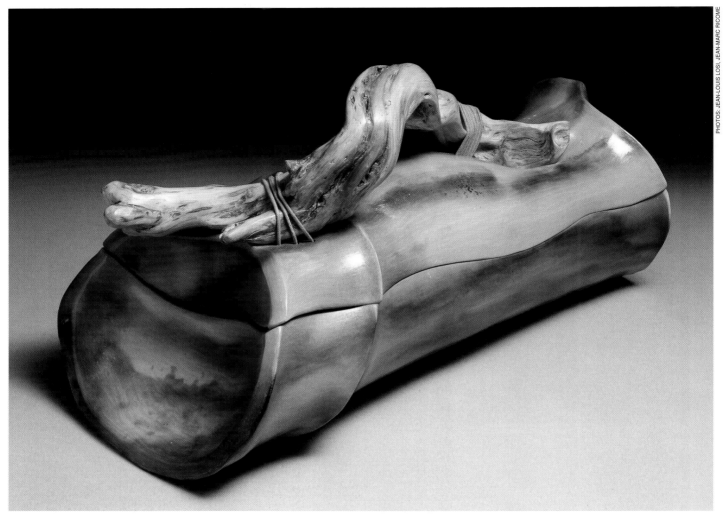

"Boit bamboo," approximately 15 inches long, handbuilt stoneware box, burnished and smoked, with driftwood handle and leather ties.

French artist Jean-Luc Mas creates burnished and smoked stoneware sculpture and vessels. Trained in graphic design, Mas worked in advertising for ten years before turning to clay. Today, he still begins by sketching ideas on paper, then constructs the basic shapes with slabs cut in large strips.

"Cylindrical shapes (machines, animals) are formed around pieces of wood with different diameters," Mas explained. "They can then be distorted or attached to other parts."

When leather hard, the forms are burnished "with the back of a little spoon to obtain a good polish. Sometimes, I use blades."

The completely dry forms are fired for 10 hours to 1000°C (1832°F) in a gas-fueled fiber kiln, before smoking individually in sawdust. Results vary, depending on the amount of flame and smoke. "To get colors exactly where I want them," Mas also lays pieces of wood and paper alongside the piece, and directs air to specific areas with a hand-held hairdryer. ▲

"Le petit poisson baleine," approximately 15 inches in diameter, burnished and smoked stoneware bottle.

"La chasse au papillon," approximately 36 inches in height, stoneware and mixed media.

"La machine à remonter le temps," approximately 32 inches in height, handbuilt and burnished stoneware, leather and wood.

Box with hinged lid, approximately 10 inches in diameter, burnished and smoked stoneware, with wood, stone and leather, by Jean-Luc Mas, Paris.

Earthenware bowl, 12 inches in height, burnished, bisqued, broken, sawdust fired, accented with torched sawdust, and reassembled.

Kevin Nierman

by David Brin

At the age of 40, Kevin Nierman still has a boyish quality about him, and when he says that all he's done his adult life is play with clay, one can almost believe it. He brings a youthful enthusiasm to his work, believing that the artist's creative side needs to be cared for and nurtured like a child.

When he was a boy, Nierman painted and repainted the walls of his room, built sculptures in the house and experimented with all kinds of decorations. "More than anything, I got an unspoken message from my mother that it's valuable to create, to play," he recalls. "She gave me the tools,

Kevin Nierman maintains a working/teaching studio in Berkeley, California; teaching children has encouraged him to "bring that playful part of myself" to his own work.

she gave me enough structure to keep me focused, she gave me the materials, and then she let me go."

As a teenager, Nierman experimented

with painting and sculpture, then started making pots when he was 22. His first teacher was Carol Robinson. When he first saw Robinson's sawdust-fired pottery, "it was as if I'd come home. Her pots are primitive, ancient looking. I felt as if I had been in the desert all my life, and suddenly there was something I resonated with so deeply. I just knew this was it."

After a six-week class with Robinson at the Colson School of Art, Nierman built a potter's wheel, bought an old kiln and set up a studio in the vestibule of his apartment in Sarasota, Florida. "I spent hours and

Wheel-thrown pot, broken and reassembled, 15 inches in height, raku fired.

hours just throwing pots. I worked a long, long time by myself, in my studio, experimenting—I'm not the kind of person who can reach out and get a lot of advice or information. Because I didn't get much formal training, something in me didn't ask questions of other people, or connect with other potters. But because I worked for so long, all of that eventually started to come to me—more information, more connection.

"What amazes me now is that I kept going for all those years. I think it was because there is something in me that has to create. I have to work with my hands, and I have a deep, deep love of clay. There was something naïve about me. I just continued to play with clay."

As he "played," Nierman's vessel style changed, but he retained his interest in the use of smoke in some form or another—through raku, pit or sawdust firing. "Because I limited myself for a

long time to unglazed vessels, I pushed the edges of smoke," Nierman explains. For example, he sometimes burns "sawdust right on the pot. I hold the pot sideways, then I take a propane torch to it. After I burn my fingers and start my shoelaces on fire, I put another bit of sawdust on the pot, and I torch that, all the way around, until the whole thing is done."

Of course, he's joking about the burnt shoelaces. He actually approaches his work much more seriously. "It takes hours and hours to do one pot. Then I look at it and decide if I want more smoke somewhere. I can control the pattern somewhat by the amount of sawdust I use. And I can get some color variation depending on the kind of sawdust and clay body."

Burnishing yields other effects. When the pots are almost dry, Nierman rubs them with a special stone that was given

to him by Blue Corn, a Native American potter. For a high shine, he then applies vegetable oil and burnishes again.

The burnished pots are bisqued in the kiln, then put upside down in a pit or a garbage can and fired slowly with wood, cow dung or sawdust. That's what creates the smoky patterns overall.

Nierman recently began breaking pots, smoking the pieces separately, then gluing them back together, so that the pot seems to be whole and in pieces at the same time. Nierman credits Rick Dillingham, a New Mexico potter who died in December 1993, with developing the technique. "I always loved Rick's work," comments Nierman. "I wouldn't crack pots for years and years, because it was Rick's thing, and I didn't want to copy him."

But Nierman's attitude changed when he was commissioned to make a large cauldron, and at the very end of the process, it cracked. "I was heartbroken. When I told the woman who had commissioned it, she said, 'So what?' So I fired it and then glued it back together. And this was my way in. I realized that what Rick Dillingham did was offer all of us a technique, and it's one that appeals to me."

Now, after the bisque firing, Nierman puts down a towel and breaks the pots right on the cement floor of his studio. "Once I hear them crack, I get nervous. I've intentionally destroyed what I've made. I know the vessel's not whole any more," he explains.

The pieces are then raku or pit fired, or torch and sawdust fired. Sometimes he uses all three firing techniques on a single pot. Afterward, the parts are glued together with epoxy.

There is no way to tell exactly how a pot is going to break, just like there is no way to exercise complete control over the ethereal patterns of smoke. For Nierman, giving up some control and allowing chance to take its course is part of the creative process. ▲

PLAYING WITH FIRE:
Experimental kilns and related firing methods

Potters are a playful bunch, always ready to experiment, invent wild and wonderful new techniques, and take advantage of the happy accident. Once we progress beyond a fear of firing, the greatest fun for a potter is that of trying out new ways of firing pots. Sometimes these new methods are developed as an answer to a vexing problem, such as how to fire something too large or fragile to lift; sometimes as a way to get around a lack of equipment; and sometimes just to see if it can be done. An experimental firing method may not be the most practical way to make pots for sale, but it can be ideal for a workshop or a group firing situation where the experience rather than the product is the most important element. After all, pit firing, used to advantage by so many potters, was once an experimental technique used primarily in workshops.

The firing techniques discussed in this chapter range from the small scale of barbecue and fireplace firing, to the large scale of the paper kiln. Will and Kate Jacobson saw a glaze flaw that developed during a raku firing as an opportunity to turn their pottery in a new direction; Bennett Bean revels in breaking the "rules" of pottery by mixing glaze, pit firing, acrylic paint, and gold leaf. Richard Behrens offers suggestions for vapor glazing in a saggar, as a way for the electric kiln owner to rediscover the joy of unpredictability. The final article, about low-fire-salt fuming, brings us full circle—for the author, Paul Soldner, was one of the pioneers of the raku movement, which spawned the development of pit and saggar firing. Salt is the primary volatile material added to most pits and saggars, therefore the next logical step after saggar firing was to omit the saggar and combustibles and fill the kiln with salt fumes alone.

By asking "what if" questions, looking for the silver lining in every cloud, and not taking themselves too seriously, potters playing with fire have developed the myriad variations of pit, barrel and saggar firing. As this process continues, new ways of combining the elements of earth, air, water and fire will ever lead to the creation of interesting, intriguing and inspiring works of ceramic art.

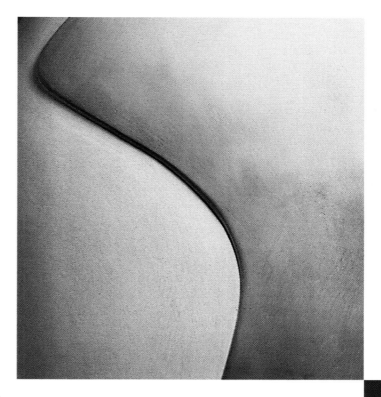

A Paper Kiln

by Caroline Court

During a year's residence in Lisbon, I had the opportunity to work with Aline Favre, a Swiss ceramist and inventor (with Christian Danthe and Fabienne Gloria) of the paper kiln. For 25 years a professor at L'Ecole des Arts Décoratifs in Geneva, Favre was in Portugal to teach at the Centro de Arte e Communicaçāo (AR˙CO).

Over the years, she has searched for the best materials and processes with which to express herself and her commitment to three-dimen-sional form. In 1977, Favre took her first steps with porcelain, and a year later won a gold medal with Florent Zeller at Faenza in recognition for their work in colored porcelain. A 1980 trip to the United States, where she worked with Paul Soldner and Jim Romberg, opened the door to raku and fumed clay.

The paper kiln was invented in 1983 to fulfill the need for a simple but effective technique for firing ce-ramics in the Jura Mountains of Switzerland. It allowed campers to participate in kiln construction and to gain an awareness of the different stages of firing. Besides, it was just plain fun, with a lot of the hands-on excitement and mystery of tradi-tional primitive firing.

In fact, traditional firing tech-niques used in Africa and the Americas were Favre's first source of inspiration. While understanding them is crucial to learn-ing the stages of firing, it is also neces-sary to adapt to local climate and available materials. Favre and her col-laborators decided to try using slurry-coated paper as insulation, as well as to protect the chamber and ware from ad-verse weather conditions.

Editor's Note: *It is essential that any-one wishing to construct a "paper kiln" first be well versed in kiln safety practices. A lightweight, minimally insulated firing chamber might become a substantial fire hazard if constructed near combustibles, in areas where wind could lead to loss of structural integrity, or where the kiln might pose an "attractive hazard" to adult visi-tors and curious children.*

Many varieties of the paper kiln have been developed since those early experiments. The following de-scribes one construction/firing that took place at AR˙CO on the first day of February 1991—a typical winter day in Portugal with bone-chilling rains alternating with intense, renewing sunshine.

Both bisque- and greenware were to be fired. As the breakage rate can be catastrophic when direct flame hits ware, it is best to work with a thermal-shock-resistant clay body high in talc and grog.

The kiln's foundation course was made of hard firebrick (about 35) set on edge and pressed into the

Flames shoot from a tin-can chimney as the large, slurry-coated-paper kiln at Centro de Arte e Communicaçāo in Portugal reaches temperature.

A paper kiln begins with a foundation of hard firebrick laid in a radiating pattern, each brick set on edge about 3 to 5 inches from the next. Charcoal is poured between the bricks and salt sprinkled overall. Once the top surfaces

have been brushed off, ware is stacked, with larger pieces straddling the bricks first. At the foundation perimeter, four openings are constructed from brick and broken kiln shelves to serve as firemouths and air-intake parts.

loosened dirt. These were laid in a radiating pattern, each brick spaced 3 to 5 inches from the next. This 60-inch-diameter foundation functioned as both the kiln floor on which ware was seated, as well as a grate to feed the fire with oxygen.

At the perimeter of the foundation, four openings were constructed from bricks and odd bits of kiln shelving; these would serve as firemouths and air intakes.

Charcoal was poured between the bricks and into the firemouths to a height of 3 inches; 3 kilograms (8 lbs.) of salt were sprinkled overall. At low temperatures, salt accentuates metal oxide colors, rendering subtle tones according to firing atmosphere (reduction or oxidation).

Oxides, sulfates and nitrates—soluble metal colorants—yield a variety of hues. Favre's favorite engobe is 50% white slip and 50% lead

bisilicate (or for safety—a boron frit) with either 3% copper carbonate or 2% cobalt carbonate added.

The ware was stacked on top of the brick grate foundation—larger pieces first, often straddling several bricks, and smaller pieces inside the larger ones. All were separated from each other by wadding (clay mixed with vermiculite) or cubes cut from firebrick. This was to allow adequate circulation and, hopefully, encourage the development of rich, interesting surfaces.

So it was that the kiln substructure was constructed from the very clay objects that were to be fired. Pieces of charcoal were placed, tucked, mounded and scattered in and about the ware. In addition, 2 kilos (5⅓ lb) of common salt were sprinkled over the entire mound.

Then the students proceeded to lean stick after stick of hardwood against the mound until the stacked

ware was visually obscured. The diameter and dryness determine how quickly and easily the sticks will burn. These factors have to be evaluated (along with expected weather conditions) for each firing when deciding what type of wood to use.

Around the wooden tepee, chicken wire was wrapped and fastened to itself with wire ties. Additional sticks were worked inside the chicken wire from the top alongside the chimney opening.

Students then prepared to cover the wire with a paper shell. They had already prepared a wheelbarrow full of yogurt-consistency slurry and had accumulated a tall stack of slick paper, as found in fashion and news magazines.

A large tin can with both ends cut out was positioned at the highest point to serve as the chimney.

From ground to chimney top, the

After additional pieces of charcoal and salt are tucked/sprinkled in and around the stacked ware, varying lengths of hardwood are leaned vertically against

the ware until all clay is visually obscured. A stretch of chicken wire is then cut long enough to wrap around this wooden tepee.

Playing With Fire

Once the chicken wire has been fastened together with wire ties, additional sticks are worked inside from the top.

A shell of slick paper (from magazines) dipped in yogurt-consistency slurry is laid over the chicken wire.

A large tin can with both ends removed is positioned at the top to serve as the kiln's chimney.

wire structure was layered with paper coated on both sides with slurry. In all, ten layers of paper were hung alternately, horizontal and vertical, with overlapping seams. The sheets at the top were folded and snuggled up against the chimney to form a heavier collar.

Once the kiln had been brushed all over with a final coat of slurry, it was ready to be fired up. There was no need to wait for the slurry to dry. Favre says she has even fired successfully in the rain.

Sometime before, a small wood fire had been started to the side, and shovelfuls of the glowing coals were placed in each of the four firemouths. As I put my hand to the kiln wall, I felt the dampness of water vapor escaping from the slurry and the heat increasing. This would

turn out to be a slow firing, taking about six hours to red-orange heat.

After the fire was well established, there wasn't much more to do except enjoy the flame and sparks shooting up into the darkness, and chat with Favre about her past and future firings.

She talked about the many variations of the paper kiln that have been developed. One involved constructing a site-specific sculpture around 2×4s driven vertically into the ground, with an air vent built into the base; it was then surrounded by more fuel (wood) and a paper shell to be fired on site.

Another variation used for firing smaller pieces had the ware piled directly over chicken wire on a metal grate elevated 3 feet above the ground (a stack of bricks support-

ing each corner); the ware and grate were then covered with wood, wire and slurry-dipped paper.

A pre-heating fire was lit in a shallow hole beneath, then the grate was lowered progressively by removing equal numbers of bricks from each corner. After the grate was flush to the ground for a few hours, a reducing flame appeared.

Favre noted that the firing at AR·CO had been a large one as paper kilns go. As kiln size increases, so does the difficulty of controlling rate-of-heat increase and evenness.

She delights in the knowledge that since the paper kiln was first attempted eight years ago, the design has continued to be refined and the technique has spread to places where it might otherwise be difficult to fire ceramics. ▲

Ten layers of slurry-coated paper are hung with overlapping seams. Around the chimney, sheets of paper are folded to form a heavy collar. Finally, a thick coat of slurry is applied over the entire kiln surface. A small fire (started nearby earlier in the day) provides shovelfuls of coals to be placed in each of the four

firemouths; this ignites the wood inside. There is no need to wait for the slurry to dry before initiating firing; paper kilns can fire even in the rain. The kiln shown here took about six hours to reach red-orange heat.

Barbecue and Fireplace Firing

by Mollie Poupeney

In the prehistoric world was the reality of clay, the magic of hands to form it, and the mystery of fire. Curiosity, and the willingness to take a risk, were two important elements that inspired early inventors of the primitive kiln to produce the ceramic forms we admire in museums today. From this beginning, the knowledge of clay has evolved into a complex technology that baffles new ceramics students who encounter the "need" for wheels, expensive or complex kilns, and higher education in order to proceed. Yet even today in much of the world the simple stone age process continues to exist as a viable and functional tradition. Folk potters in Africa, Mexico, Middle and South America, as well as Indians of the American Southwest, have been recognized for their artistry in producing handbuilt ware fired in dung or open bonfire kilns.

The urban or suburban potter with a desire to use an open fire will find that adapting primitive methods to a populated area and stay-

ing within local fire and environmental regulations is *easier* than it may seem. The backyard barbecue or a fireplace, fueled with combustibles such as charcoal briquettes, can be used to fire clay.

While a variety of bodies may be successful, typical earthenware is best adapted to this method when mixed with thirty to forty per cent sand or grog to withstand the shock of fast rising temperature. To more completely experience the process, local clay may be dug, perhaps in that part of the garden where nothing grows readily. Clay which can be formed and dried in one piece will generally fire. Sieved fireplace ashes, sawdust, coffee grounds, and other body fillers can be added to clay for additional drying and firing stability.

Small pots may be formed by any method and should be air dried, then thoroughly dried by placing on a floor heating register, in an oven, or on the food grate of a barbecue. The ware is taken directly from warming to the fuel grate of the barbecue, surrounded

A lidded barbecue may be used as a kiln and fired with charcoal briquettes.

Playing With Fire

1. In preparation for firing, charcoal briquettes are poured onto the fuel grate.

2. Preheated ware is placed among the briquettes. The pot wrapped in paper and foil will be carbonized.

5. Blackware may be produced by firing with combustibles inside a lidded can.

6. To simultaneously fire a number of pots, slices of pressed fuel logs provide additional heat.

with charcoal for even heating and insulation, soaked with charcoal lighter, and ignited. Pots can be removed after a half hour in the red heat of the coals, or left until completely cold.

Depending upon how the ware is placed, its surface effects will vary. When fired among the briquettes, body color will range from shaded tan, red, and brown to gray and black. For an overall terra-cotta color, ware can be fired in an unlidded tin can to protect it from direct contact with the flame. Wrapping a pot in paper towels or newspaper and then putting it in a lidded metal can or enclosing it in several layers of heavy-duty aluminum foil will produce a contained, smoky atmosphere during firing, and thus the carbonized finish characteristic of traditional blackware. If the pot is burnished prior to drying, it will have a glossy surface after firing.

There are many usable styles of barbecues and suitable fuels. The enclosed, cylindrical smoker comes closest to duplicating kiln construction, while barbecues with lids and vents make safe, contained fires possible if

3. Charcoal lighter can be applied overall without damaging smaller pots.

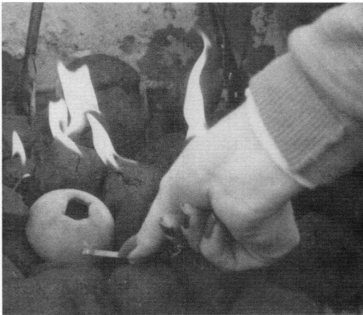

4. The barbecue is lit and allowed to burn until the ware glows with dull red heat.

7. When placed over the ware chamber, the fuel helps insulate the can against excessive heat loss.

8. The barbecue's lid and vents regulate draft and increase available heat.

fuels are used which do not emit a great deal of flame. As skill with this method increases and larger pots are fired, a fireplace may provide more space for ware.

Small amounts of wood bark or pressed sawdust log slices produce very hot fires and a temporarily carbonaceous atmosphere in an enclosed barbecue; the smoke can be regulated by opening or closing the lid. Potters with access to dried dung fuel may use similar firing procedures. Adequate amounts of both fuel and firing time will sufficiently harden the ware, but if the clay can be scratched easily with a nail, or appears crumbly, refire with more fuel and for a longer time.

Remember that the first potters had no teachers—only the mud beneath their feet, the magic of their hands, and the mystery of flame. They did well, and so will you. ▲

9. Unglazed ware may make contact during firing. Burnishing when green produces the glossy finish.

10. Ware may be preheated on the food grate of a hot barbeque or in a regular kitchen oven.

11. Smoke cookers such as this are also usable for firing pots among the coals.

Left, above: Larger pots can be preheated near wood embers in a fireplace or Franklin stove.

Left: Pressed log fuel slices are arranged around and over large ware, then lit, and burned.

Above: Fired coil pot, 11 inches in height, by the author.

Will and Kate Jacobson (Shelton, Washington) said good-bye to "manufacturing" in order to return to basics.

Freedom to Discover

by Will and Kate Jacobson

As potters, we once wholeheartedly subscribed to the doctrine of utilitarianism, which was the vehicle for financial stability in our production studio. But, over the last several years, we have dramatically altered our view.

The transition began when we realized the production business had somehow transformed us from potters to manufacturers. Somewhere between purchase-order deadlines and workers compensation insurance we forgot why we had become potters. We were marketing to over 300 wholesale accounts and retailing at 25 craft shows a year. We had a computer to keep track of our files—our pottery had become merchandise, numbers and units. What began as a labor of love became just labor.

As we improved technically over the years, it seemed our work was losing a sense of self-expression, creativity and joy that drew us to working in clay. Usefulness became an obstacle. Even technical proficiency became a trap. During our neophyte years, clay was the medium for our art. When clay became a business, we lost the fundamental determinant of any art form: the freedom to explore, to experiment, to make mistakes and to pursue the happy accident.

If all we had wanted out of life was financial security, we would have become mid-level functionaries and ac-

quired enough wealth to afford to vote Republican. Something had to change. We chose to rediscover the art in our craft.

Touring the country with retail craft fairs gave us the opportunity to see diverse contemporary art. In each city, we investigated the local art scene. Museums and galleries were great sources for new ideas, but exchanging thoughts with other artists had the greatest impact on broadening our attitudes.

Coming from a functional point of view, we had built mental walls (restrictions) concerning the acceptable parameters of clay. A cup, for instance, could only be made within certain size limitations and remain useful. But there are no pottery police who write citations for illegal use of clay or for parking your acrylic paint on a pot without a permit.

We were determined to create work that reflected our new consciousness, trying anything that came to mind. We willfully wasted time that could have been spent producing salable ceramic goods.

Of course, creativity can be a good deal less lucrative than functionalism and repetition. Even when our explorations ended in artistic success, that did not necessarily mean economic success. For instance, at one point we were experimenting with low-fire salt

techniques. Although we and other potters considered them to be phenomenally great pots, we couldn't find a market for them. Also, fully 70% were laid to rest through frustration therapy—throwing them at the dumpster from 20 feet away.

Finally, we found something new and exciting. We were experimenting with colored slips underneath raku glazes, when we noticed a small part of the glaze had flaked off one of our test pots. What was happening under the glaze seemed to be of interest, so we used a knife to scrape all the remaining glaze off the pot, then scrubbed with steel wool.

Rather than dismissing this as a glaze flaw, we consider it a new decorating process. We brush a slip onto bisqued work, let it dry, then apply glaze. As the glaze melts, it fuses to the slip and is prevented from reaching the pot. After traditional raku postfiring reduction, the glaze can be peeled off the pot. The resulting thick shadow lines show where the carbon seeped through the outside glaze layer. We have found we can create a batik effect by layering glaze in repeated firings. Figurative work can be drawn through the glaze, and a reverse image can be achieved with carbon saturation. It took us nearly two years to develop this process sufficiently to reliably control the outcome. The

Above: "Spirals,"
20 inches in height.

Left: After a Cone
012–010 bisque
firing, each pot is
covered with slip
made from 40%
Lincoln 60 fireclay,
30% 6-Tile clay, 20%
Ione 412 grog and
10% Custer feldspar;
then glazed with a
mixture of 60% Ferro
frit 3110 and 40%
Gerstley borate; fired
to Cone 014; smoked;
water quenched;
and peeled.

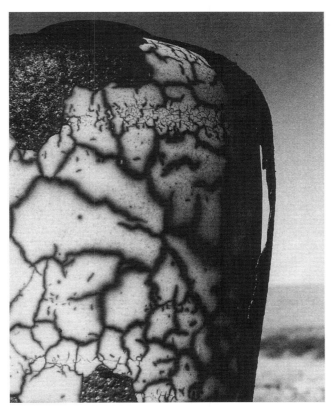

Smoke penetrating the layer of fused slip and glaze creates random carbon patterning that follows crack lines.

As the eggshell-like layer of slip and glaze is loosened, large sheets begin to fall away.

potential applications seem endless. [Also see Jerry Caplan's "Raku Reduction Stenciling" in the November 1976 CM.]

Maintaining a sense of wonder about our work is absolutely crucial. The freedom to experiment and explore new forms or techniques is a necessary part of our lives. But it is difficult—particularly for potters—to balance creative exploration and economic independence. It is easy to get caught up in the day-to-day routine of repeating successful designs and processes. Our markets perpetuate repetition. Potters share a problem with other artists in that even progressive galleries tend to buy work they've sold in the past and are often wary of new designs.

Creative marketing now helps us maintain a balance between aesthetics and economics. In addition to our net-30 accounts, we have a few galleries with which we work on a consignment basis. We allow our net-30 customers to order from samples and to specify (within reason) the finished work. Our more experimental work goes to consignment galleries.

While artists in other media don't have the initial financial security offered by utilitarianism, neither are they as likely to be seduced (by technical skill and economic success) into just manufacturing. At the same time, it's hard to imagine completely abandoning utilitarianism. There's something very special about a well-made bowl. It feels good to make something both beautiful and useful. There is comfort in the knowledge that we are continuing an ancient and noble tradition. But we also know that clay is a uniquely plastic medium of communication and expression—and there comes a time when technical expertise becomes something to master and transcend.

After all, art and craft, artist and artisan, are just labels that don't have to be kept cleanly compartmentalized. We prefer to approach our craft as artists, with the freedom to explore and fail occasionally and, most importantly, the freedom to discover. ▲

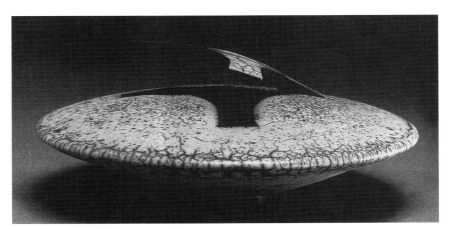

"Gateway," 12 inches in diameter, a closed form thrown from raku clay, with cut and lifted handlelike element, bisqued, covered with slip/glaze, smoked and peeled.

Playing With Fire

Untitled teapot, 7 inches in height, pit-fired earthenware, with glaze, acrylics, white gold leaf and epoxy.

Bennett Bean
Playing by His Rules
by Karen S. Chambers

"**A**t the beginning of the Renaissance, painting was not art," muses New Jersey artist Bennett Bean, as he talks about his 30-year-plus career as a potter, painter, sculptor, designer, furniture-maker, teacher." Painters were hired by the Church to paint paintings that were used as teaching devices to bring the word of God to the unlettered. They were put out of business, lost their socio-economic niche, with the arrival of the printing press. Then the activity became available as art."

Bean was holding forth in the living room of the 18th-century farmhouse he has shared for 27 years with his wife, Cathy Bao, a former professor of philosophy: "Essentially, the same thing happened with ceramics. Potters were put out of business by plastics, tin, alu-minum. They lost their spot, so ceramics became available for art. Now, the mistake that most people make is that they think the content of ceramics should be the same as art; it should be art in clay. But there are characteristics in ceramics that are totally of that universe. The basic one is the vessel."

For Bean, the "real distinction between art and non-art is content, not material, not style." He explains that the subject of his ceramic work, "the same way a painting has a subject, comes from the traditional vessel. I'm not making pieces about use, volume, tactility, narrative. My pieces, since about 1980, are specifically about decorated surfaces outside and space inside."

But Bean's work is hardly simple. The decoration has become increasingly complex as he plays the organic effects of pit firing against areas of translucent glaze, bright acrylic paint and luminous gilding. He no longer makes utilitarian pots, but instead constructs dynamic tableaux of sliced-open, wheel-thrown forms with slab additions.

Bean has arrived at this point through a career-long search that began as a student at the State University of Iowa. "I was a standard undergraduate art major, trying to make up my mind between painting and ceramics. The painting faculty were so self-obsessed that they were unable to communicate at all. The faculty of the ceramics department and the students were at least grounded in the world. Also, I was seduced by the technique; throwing is absolutely seductive."

Untitled ("Footed Vessel Series"), 17 inches in height, glazed earthenware, pit fired, with acrylics on the exterior and gold leaf applied to the interior.

Although Bean took 13 semesters of drawing during his academic career, he majored in ceramics, earning a B.A. degree in 1963. He began his graduate work at the University of Washington, where Fred Bauer and Patti Warashina were fellow students, but left after one semester to study with Paul Soldner at Claremont College in Southern California, receiving an M.F.A. in 1966. Then, as part of the last generation of graduate students to be assured a teaching post, Bean was hired by Wagner College on Staten Island to teach ceramics, as well as a variety of other craft and design courses, and sculpture.

He found himself in the middle of the fine-art world. "It seemed impossible to do ceramics there, so I thought what do people do in New York? Well, they do art, so I started making art."

Bean began making acrylic-and-Plexiglas sculptures in the California version of minimalism called "Cool Art,"

and six months later sold a piece to the Whitney Museum of American Art. After his work was included in the prestigious Whitney Biennial in 1968, he was picked up by a major commercial gallery specializing in contemporary fine art. But this immediate success "was quite a shock to my system. It seemed to me that you were supposed to labor in the vineyards of anonymity for years and slowly be recognized. Well, I showed up in New York, read a book, and literally was seized upon by the establishment," Bean recounts. "I looked at this with a somewhat jaundiced view. By 1970 I had had enough of that universe, thought that the clay subculture was filled with much nicer people and that I would return to that world."

That was the year Bean found a colonial farmhouse near the Delaware Water Gap in New Jersey that his wife says was "suffering from benign neglect." After moving to the farm, he returned

to throwing pots, picking up where he left off in graduate school, "making Bizen-influenced Japanese pots. Since then, it has been a slow evolution to the work that I'm doing now. It was very much a step at a time."

The house was within commuting distance to Staten Island, where he continued to teach until 1978, although his tenure was a stormy one. The administration fired Bean three times, but he was reinstated each time. The final time, he was given what he refers to as a "terminal sabbatical," during which he realized that he could make more money and have a better time as a full-time practicing artist.

It was on the occasion of the second firing attempt in 1974 that, as Bean tells the story, "I thought I would have to make a living. The economy had gone in the hole and I had never thought of the economy collapsing before. I had just never considered the economy." When he was growing up in Iowa City, where his father was the head of the department of internal medicine at the state university, "checks came 12 times a year no matter what the economy was doing, so I thought, 'Oh my God, a depression is coming and I've got to make something that is completely depression-proof.' The only thing I could think of was death; hence the 'Burial Urn' series," an exploration of Chinese celadons and Song-dynasty forms.

This interest in Oriental ceramics, still pervasive in Western ceramics communities at the time, led to a 1975 series of flameware sake warmers. With these, Bean realized that a work was not necessarily finished when it came out of the kiln. "I was doing flameware and I was doing lusters, because the flameware didn't have enough visual strength. It was matt and brown; it was like 'let's get a little more oomph out of this deal.'"

In the spirit of experimentation and curiosity that characterizes his career, he wondered what would happen if he "just painted the lusters on and fired them with a torch. I went outside where I wouldn't die from luster fumes and painted it, fired it with a torch, looked at it, realized it wasn't good, added

141

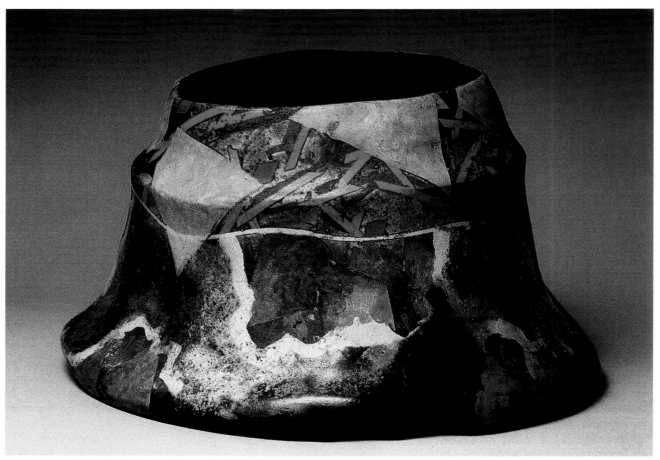

Untitled vessel, 7 inches in height, pit-fired earthenware, with acrylics and black latex, by Bennett Bean, Blairstown, New Jersey.

sections, fired it again with a torch. A lot of it was impatience, because a luster firing is a 12- or 14-hour process. Now I can do six luster firings in 20 minutes, and keep adding, keep embellishing."

That discovery made him conclude that "they lied to me in graduate school. They said when the thing came out of the kiln, it was permanent, it would be that way for 2000 years." He saw that post-firing techniques could be used to get the effects he envisioned. "My expectations and what I was getting back from the kiln were not always the same. This was an effort to get the last word."

This experience led to a series that began in 1975 in which Bean airbrushed designs onto the fired surface of platters using semivitreous slips. The compositions were partially inspired by the works of the post-painterly abstractionist Larry Poons, who arranged geometric motifs in a regular pattern on the picture plane. This exploration was the beginning of what has become Bean's signature look, a formal dialogue of hard-edged geo-

metric motifs versus more organic effects resulting from wood firing.

These works clearly mark an abandonment of the Oriental heritage that no longer seemed appropriate to Bean. He looked, instead, closer to home, admiring Native American ceramics and collecting American art pottery. Bean also began to explore postfiring decorative effects, such as the sheen that Native American potters achieved by rubbing the surface of a fired pot with an animal skin impregnated with fat. He adapted the process, first using linseed oil and now paste urethane.

To add color after firing, Bean began by using various colorants, including ocher, which he thought would be marginally acceptable to ceramics purists. Opting not to be restricted by tradition, he soon turned to other materials, experimenting with various paints before choosing acrylic in 1982.

Another more traditional postfiring technique that Bean uses is gilding. This began in 1983 when he started apply-

ing gold leaf in response to a desire to use the open vessel form, without relinquishing the basic tenet of his aesthetic exploration: decorated surface outside, space inside. "I saw some Mimbres bowls and thought I'd like to make that shape. It's such a wonderful shape. But as soon as I made that shape, it became skin outside and skin inside. I'd lost my space. It was surface inside and surface outside. The space had opened out. The problem was finding a material that read as space, and gold did that."

Why Bean felt compelled to resolve this issue in this manner is explained by his intellectual process of creation: "Construct yourself a universe, based on some ideas that you're interested in and make rules around those ideas—I'll do this; I won't do that. Once you have those rules, it's like a sonnet. It's a very clear, very rational structure, and within that rational structure, you have complete freedom to play."

For Bean, following the rules is a very creative process. ▲

Untitled ("Triple Series"), 15 inches in height, wheel-thrown and altered earthenware, with masked glazes, pit fired, accented with acrylics and gold leaf.

Making a Bean Pot

Bennett Bean's richly decorated earthenware forms are complicated visually and technically, taking nearly 20 steps and combining traditional and nontraditional ceramic processes. It is a long process but a way of working that "is entirely appropriate to my neuroses," Bean says.

He begins by throwing a group of vessels from a white earthenware body. When they are leather hard, he burnishes them with a stainless-steel rod to remove the throwing marks. He then arranges two or more vessels into a composition where each part relates to the other in a dialogue of forms, sometimes cutting them apart and overlapping the sections or adding extensions. When thoroughly dry, they are brushed with white terra sigillata and polished, then fired to Cone 06.

Bean then masks off areas using Chartpak Pressure Sensitive Graphic Tape, Contact paper or wax. His glazes—made of equal parts (by volume) Mason stain, Pemco frit P25 and 20 Mule Team Borax—are mixed to a thin consistency and painted on like watercolor. "This glaze is designed to go in a pit and get hard enough to stay on the pot, but no so gooey that the ashes and crud from the pit stick to it," Bean explains.

The pots are pit fired with dry wood, but the wood smoke imparts a gray, not the deep black that Bean wants. That comes from the addition of green hardwood sawdust and oats. Salt and copper cause the pink blushes. Wearing heat-resistant gloves, Bean can rearrange the pots during the firing to control and effects. The heat of the wood fire burns off the tape and melts the wax, leaving white areas.

Usually, his assistant, Jane Clark, gilds the interiors and other designated areas. Then, using acrylic, Bean paints the remaining masked areas. One of his "rules" is to paint only the unglazed areas. But, if necessary to make the composition work, he will paint over the glaze. The entire piece is then sealed inside and out with urethane gel. Multipart forms are mounted on matt black wooden slabs to control how they are seen by viewers.

Bean does not make detailed drawings for his pieces, although he does make "shorthand notes to myself. When I'm working on these pieces, I am not planning on the future. When I work on the green clay, I'm making green clay shapes. I'm not thinking about what color the glaze is going to be or how they're going to be painted. I'm doing what I'm doing. When I get to the decoration stage, then I'm thinking about decoration as pattern, but not as color. When I get to the painting stage, I'm thinking about painting. So I'm doing exactly what I'm doing when I'm doing it. I've made the rules."

Playing With Fire

Vapor Glazing in a Saggar

by Richard Behrens

Observant early potters noted the tendency of some glazes to vaporize with resultant glassy deposits on the walls of their saggars. (Saggars are thick walled clay forms, usually shaped somewhat like hat boxes, which have been used as alternatives to kiln shelves, and to protect ware from direct flame and ash.) This transfer by volatilization was often diminished by coating the interior walls of the saggar with glaze so that a reciprocal and opposing flow of vapor was returned to the ware. Eventually, enterprising potters began to use this phenomenon to further advantage, firing unglazed ware in saggars painted with easily volatilized glaze compositions. When fired, the vaporizing glaze migrated to the ware, covering it with a thin, stable coating relatively free from common defects such as crazing. The lack of pooling of glaze in sharply defined contours proved to be well adapted to the production of fine-detailed ware.

Commonly used for saggar glazing techniques were glaze materials such as sodium, lithium, potassium, and boron, which volatilized at red heat and attacked the clay body, forming very stable alkali-aluminum-silicate glazes. These "smear glazes," as they were called during the past century, were suitable also for single firing, allowing the simultaneous maturing of ware and glaze.

A disadvantage of saggar firing, common to all vapor glazing, is the relatively static diffusion of vapor, making it necessary to use conventional glazes on recessed, relatively inaccessible areas such as the interiors of bottles. An advantage of particular interest to many contemporary potters is the adaptability of the technique for use in electric kilns. Those wishing to do experimental work can prepare saggars either from conventional saggar clays, or from the following mixture:

Saggar Body
Plastic Fireclay 40.0%
Calcined Fireclay 30.0
Grog 28.0
Bentonite 2.0
100.0%

This body can be thrown into round forms, or it lends itself well to the production of rectangular slab forms. Regardless of shape, the saggar needs a close-fitting (but not pneumatically tight) lid.

A highly alkaline glaze containing sodium, potassium, and lithium, often with the addition of alkali borates, is usually adaptable for vapor glazing. Chloride compounds have long been used, but have the disadvantage of releasing the irritating vapors of hydrochloric acid which may corrode metals and pollute the atmosphere. Alternatively, a vapor glazing mixture of carbonates may be employed; in this instance, the by-product is noncorrosive carbon dioxide gas. Here is a formula for a carbonate mixture which has yielded suitable results:

Carbonate Vapor Glazing Mixture
Borax 20.0%
Lithium Carbonate 27.0
Soda Ash 50.0
Bentonite 3.0
100.0%

The bentonite improves adherence of the mixture to the sides and lid of the saggar; the bottom is, of course, left uncoated.

Any good workable body may be used to produce ware for saggar glazing, although a high-silicate body is desirable, and the addition of small amounts of silica (wedged into the body) may improve effects. Interesting colors may be obtained by including in the body additions of from three to five per cent red iron oxide, copper oxide, green chrome oxide, or one of the several commercial glaze stains. Various colored slips, particularly terra sigillata, may be used to mask the underlying clay. These should have a sufficient silica content to assure good interface union between the alkaline vapors and body.

Another satisfactory means of coloration is the application of soluble colorants to the bisqued body. Sulfates, chlorides, nitrates, and acetates of various metals may be tried. Of these salts, the nitrates might be the first choice because of their ready solubility as well as the ease with which they break down when heated; nitrates of iron, copper, cobalt, nickel, manganese, and uranium are suggested. Potassium dichromate may also be tested. Twenty grams colorant per one hundred milliliters of water may serve as a guide in preparing these solutions. In the case of cobalt, a powerful colorant, five grams per one hundred milliliters seems sufficient. For application, bisque-fired ware is immersed in the desired solution for about ten seconds, or the mixture may be uniformly applied by brushing or spraying.

The firing range of the vapor glazing mixtures recommended here is generally in the Cone 4–8 area, although suitable stoneware bodies may be tested as high as Cone 12. On medium temperature, red-firing bodies, the Cone 4 range is appropriate. The potter who is interested in trying ideas could do much in changing time of firing or atmosphere in the kiln. Volatile metal dust, like zinc or bismuth, might be converted into a paste and painted on the inside of the saggar to modify the glaze appearance. The spontaneous and unpredictable nature of saggar-fired vapor glazes can yield many attractive glaze complements not generally available with electric firing. ▲

Low-Fire-Salt Fuming

by Paul Soldner

I am often asked why there isn't any written information on how to do low-fire-salt fuming. Despite the fact that it has been practiced for more than 20 years, I don't know of any books or articles giving specific directions. The following are concepts and methods I have learned mostly through trial and error.

In the beginning, it should be expected that there will be even more accidental effects from low-fire salting than ever found in raku. Perhaps this is the reason that so little information is available. Nevertheless, with experience accumulated from each firing, potters can discover what works best in their own kilns. And, yes, soda can also be fumed in the same way as salt.

The Clay Body

Almost any clay can be used in low-fire-salt fuming, but if orange-flashing effects are desired, then the body should include some iron oxide. If slips, terra sigillata or stains are to be applied to the surface, the clay body can be any stoneware, porcelain or a raku blend.

My favorite low-fire-salt body is a mixture of equal parts plastic fireclay, Kentucky ball clay (OM 4), red clay and sand (20 to 60 mesh). Note that there is an absence of flux; however, salt vapor fluxes the body, making it harder than regular bisqueware even at Cone 010.

The Kiln

Either an updraft or downdraft fuel-burning kiln can be used. Excellent results can be obtained with

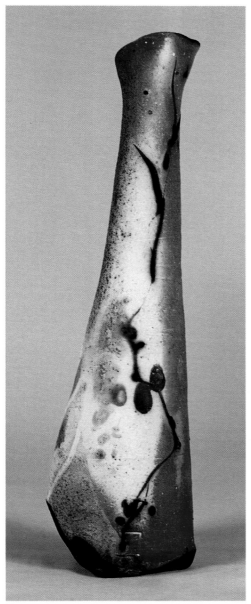

Low-fire-salt vase, 18 inches in height, thrown and altered, with slips and fumed copper.

hardbrick, softbrick, even fiber kilns, but the burner ports must enter horizontally. Kilns with bottom burners cannot be used because salt cannot be volatilized anywhere in the kiln except in the burner flame itself.

A salting port should be located directly above each burner so that salt can be dropped into the flame. Because it is important that salt fall into the flame, each burner port should be no higher than the kiln floor. If it is higher, build a salting platform level with each burner. The kiln also needs a peephole near the bottom of the door so that the quality of the atmosphere can be inspected during the firing. Finally, there must be a primary-air control on each burner.

Stacking

Effects of low-fire salting can be compared to high-temperature wood firings. Variation is enhanced by the flame moving through the ware; there is also a flame-resist effect when work is tightly stacked and touching. In some ways, flame movement is similar to the beautiful patterns produced by a river flowing under, over and through rocks. In this case, the flame is the river and the pots are the rocks.

Specific patterns can be achieved by masking surfaces with thin (approximately ⅛-inch-thick) pancakes of clay. Several layers of pages from glossy magazines or even thin slices of wood if placed under a clay pancake will produce dark gray patterns. Keep in mind that the shapes of the masking objects that touch the

Low-fire-soda, thrown-and-altered form, 27½ inches in height.

surfaces will have an effect on the patterns they leave.

Other patterns can be achieved by embedding rock salt into the clay pancake. A few large grains of salt will leave a beauty spot! Metal oxides or organic materials like seaweed can also be used.

The kiln, properly stacked for low-fire-salt fuming, will look like a disaster area to the uninformed observer. And

it will necessarily be completely full. Shelves are not only unnecessary, but actually nonproductive, as glazes are not used and the temperature is so low.

Surface Preparation

If there is a small amount of iron in the clay body, spectacular oranges, yellows and brown flashing can be expected. Raku slips will also have a positive reaction to the process. A raku

white slip containing 1 part Gerstley borate, 2 parts flint and 3 parts kaolin will often flash a beautiful pink from copper added to the salt or fumed off other copper-decorated ware. The same slip with 3%–5% copper carbonate added will be even more reactive.

Colors (from copper in particular) are often quite varied because of the complex stacking, which results in reduction-oxidation and neutral flames

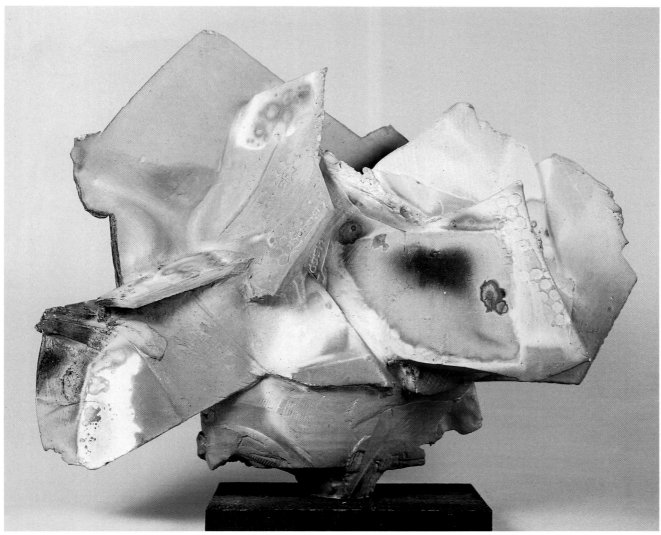

Low-fire-salt vessel sculpture, 27 inches in height, thrown and slab built.

licking over the object simultaneously. Similar variation in flashing can be anticipated from the use of terra sigillatas; however, the sigillata should be applied very thinly and/or fired to a higher temperature (possibly from Cone 06 to Cone 01) to prevent cracking. Applying the sigillata to damp bisqueware also seems to help. Remember, less planned decoration is better, and none is often good enough.

Firing

The firing cycle is approximately the same length as a bisque firing. Although stacking, surface preparation and body composition are important, it is the quality and the quantity of the flame that make low-fire-salt fuming so different from other firings. To begin, the primary air on each burner is reduced to make a long, dirty, soft yellow flame for the entire firing. Oxidation and reduction cycles of glaze firings are of little significance in the low-fire salting; however, to pull the flame through the ware, dampers need to be open throughout the entire firing.

Of utmost importance is the need to fire the kiln with excess fuel. This is determined by observing the pressure at the bottom peephole. Above 1300°F, visible flames should be exiting constantly from the peephole. If this state cannot be maintained, increase the gas, add extra burners or drill out the burner orifices until flames are obtained.

Of course, this is a reducing atmosphere, except that it is achieved with the dampers opened and the kiln drawing. Curiously, cones will change their melting point and are therefore not an exact indication of the actual temperature, but are close enough to warrant their use.

Thrown-and-altered form with slips, 6 inches in height, salt glazed in the firebox, by Paul Soldner, Aspen, Colorado.

Salting

Before loading the kiln, place salt in the flame path of each burner. A mound the size of a large orange is a good amount to start with.

When the kiln turns dull red, at about 1000°F, add more salt to each burner. For convenience, the salt can be wrapped in newspaper to form a salt "burrito," then pushed through the salting port into the flame. Additional salting every hour should be enough to achieve the desired effects.

A small amount of copper carbonate added to the salt may be helpful in encouraging a pink blush on the otherwise white slip surfaces. Many other oxides may be used to modify the fuming effects, but none as dramatically.

Oversalting may dull the surface color, so be conservative. Salting at the end of the firing is optional. Personal experience will determine its importance. Also, experiment with closing the dampers during the salting cycle, but only for a few minutes.

Work decorated with slips can be fired from Cone 010 to Cone 06. Terra-sigillata surfaces are better fired higher, from Cone 08 to Cone 3. Because there is no glaze to melt, precise temperature control is not a problem.

After the cones have melted and the last salt burrito has been added, the kiln can be shut off and cooled in the usual manner; no other treatment is needed or helpful. A good rule is to cool the kiln in the same amount of time it took to fire it.

Postfiring

In order to protect the somewhat soft surfaces, apply one or two coats of acrylic floor wax (such as Futura) diluted about half and half with water to both the inside and out. If the result is too shiny when dry, dilute the wax a little more. The coating will preserve the colors and allow the work to be cleaned by washing with water from time to time. ▲